D1027120

ADVANCE PRAISE

"If young adults could be guided in the right direction for a life journey of meaning and purpose, we would be grooming the leaders of tomorrow for a better world. This book is the perfect guide."
—Deepak Chopra, MD, FACP, founder of the Chopra Center for Wellbeing

"For those entering adulthood, purpose is fundamental to health, happiness, and creative work. Christine's guidebook is the finest map of the territory today and an inspiring picture of what purposeful living can be all about—if we dare! Read this book to experience your life in a whole new way!"
—Richard Leider, international bestselling author of *The Power of Purpose, Life Reimagined, Work Reimagined,* and *Repacking Your Bags.*

"*The Big Picture* is a researched, accessible, and practical guide that has everything young people need to figure out what to do with their lives."
—Pepper Schwartz, PhD, professor of sociology at the University of Washington and author of *Finding your Perfect Match*

"*The Big Picture* is very relevant and valuable for our youth—and I'm glad to see this initiative. Exercises like these can have a transformative impact on young adults. Indeed, purpose is an area in which we all would benefit from deeper reflection."
—Hitendra Wadhwa, professor, Columbia Business School

"Whelan's book is a must-read for those asking "what next?" in college and beyond. Building off her popular classes at the University of Wisconsin's School of Human

Ecology, *The Big Picture* is a step-by-step guide for identifying what matters to you, and how to make your mark in the world."
—Soyeon Shim, PhD, dean of the School of Human Ecology, University of Wisconsin-Madison

"This book isn't for the "I think I'll read, scratch my beard, and think" set. It's for doers. It's for people who want to live fulfilled, purposeful lives. Christine Whelan gives us a book that's grounded in both science and philosophy. It's interactive. It's fun. Most important, it's wise. I loved it."
—Victor J. Strecher, PhD, MPH, professor and director for Innovation and Social Entrepreneurship, University of Michigan School of Public Health

"*The Big Picture* is the ideal small-steps guide for young adults to reimagine their lives and seek purpose from the start. As the foremost expert in effective self-improvement, Christine Whelan offers a book that spans the generations."
—Emilio Pardo, president, Life Reimagined

"Rarely have pages in a book felt as comfortable and trustworthy as an old friend, but *The Big Picture* accomplishes that and more. Across the lifespan, understanding and implementing purpose in our lives is critical but can be daunting . . . not now! The journey to understanding your purpose now and beyond has been broken down into doable exercises and fun steps guaranteed to be a trip worth taking."
—Janet Taylor, MD, MPH Psychiatrist

"No college grad should be without this priceless wisdom. The leading expert on self-help is your guide through interactive exercises, tested advice, and powerful tools to clarify your purpose and navigate next steps. *The Big Picture* is a research-based, fun way to get past uncertainty, doubt, or nagging from your parents so you can be your best self now."
—Rich Feller, PhD, past president, National Career Development Association

"They say laughter is the best medicine, but I disagree. The real key to lifelong health and happiness is purpose.

"As a physician I have seen the power of purpose play out in the lives of people of all ages. As the father of five I know that helping young people understand what matters most is essential to their enjoyment of all that life has to offer. I'd happily prescribe this book to anyone interested in exploring meaning in their lives. Christine Whelan doesn't preach —she guides. Take this workbook on your journey as you ask what matters and how to make it happen."
—Bill Thomas, MD, founder of the Age of Disruption World Tour

"Research shows that having a purpose in life is linked to better health and better sleep—so why wait?"
—Eric Kim, PhD, Harvard School of Public Health

"Christine Whelan's *The Big Picture* should be read and experienced by every high school and college student and recommended by every parent, teacher, and mentor. At a time when so many young people are struggling to find their life's path and purpose, this wise, warm, and witty book will help to light their way forward."
—John J. DiIulio Jr., Frederic Fox Leadership Professor, University of Pennsylvania

What the Readers Say

"The Big Picture offers excellent and comforting postcollege advice that helps graduates avoid feelings of tension, anxiety, uncertainty, and worry. It does something rare: it helps the reader realize what he or she really wants in his or her life, not what society or parents want. But most importantly, this book shows young adults in a calm and collected manner how to discover the many paths they can take."
—Natalie Shribman, Bates College

"This book was a wake-up call to find my purpose in life. I thought I had it all figured out, but *The Big Picture* helped me examine my current goals and aspirations, offering a new, meaning-focused perspective."
—Joseph Mazarella, Duquesne University

"The Big Picture helped me so much more than I could have ever imagined. As I began reading, I realized that even though my real adult life hadn't started, I'd noticed that the movie of my life *had* started, and I was in it now. The camera is rolling, and I'm ready for it—wherever it takes me. This book is helping me direct it."
—Nico Galván, The New School

"I honestly could have never gotten to where I am today without having worked through this book. It really made me think of my goals, dreams, values, and purpose. It made me think of how I want to live for the rest of my life, not only focusing on the short term but the long. Any kids who don't know what they want to do with their lives should read this book."
—Robert Hillard, University of Pittsburgh

"I was not expecting that *The Big Picture* would teach me anything about myself, but it actually illustrated a lot about my priorities and showed me just how much legacy matters to me. I recently changed from premed to prelaw. I was confident in my decision at the time, but still had a few doubts that prelaw was the right move. This book helped cement my feeling that I made the right move."
—Hugh Hamilton, University of Pennsylvania

"The Big Picture is a relatable book that meets us where we are right now. It helped me reflect on my skills and values in a meaningful way—and then guided me toward action for a purposeful life as a college student and beyond. The exercises will help you get down to the heart of the matter and then, through personal exploration, begin to branch out to the larger purpose and goals."
—Ally Tufenkjian, New York University

"This book has made me more motivated to do something with my life starting *right now*. I've considered more careers than I had originally, too, because I want to do something that makes me feel good about my impact on the world. Plus, reading this book helped me limit my stress a bit. Whew!"
—Nikki Burnett, University of Pittsburgh

The Big Picture

the BIG Picture

A GUIDE TO FINDING YOUR PURPOSE IN LIFE

CHRISTINE B. WHELAN, PhD

TEMPLETON PRESS

Templeton Press
300 Conshohocken State Road, Suite 500
West Conshohocken, PA 19428
www.templetonpress.org

© 2016 by Christine B. Whelan

All rights reserved. No part of this book may be used or reproduced,
stored in a retrieval system, or transmitted in any form or by any means,
electronic, mechanical, photocopying, recording, or otherwise,
without the written permission of Templeton Press.

Designed and typeset by Gopa & Ted2, Inc.

Author photo credit: Nicole Krueger, Vintage Pear Photography

Library of Congress Cataloging-in-Publication Data on file

Printed in the United States of America

21 22 23 24 25   10 9 8 7 6 5 4 3 2

For Daniel Whelan Moyers

Contents

Ally's Big Picture

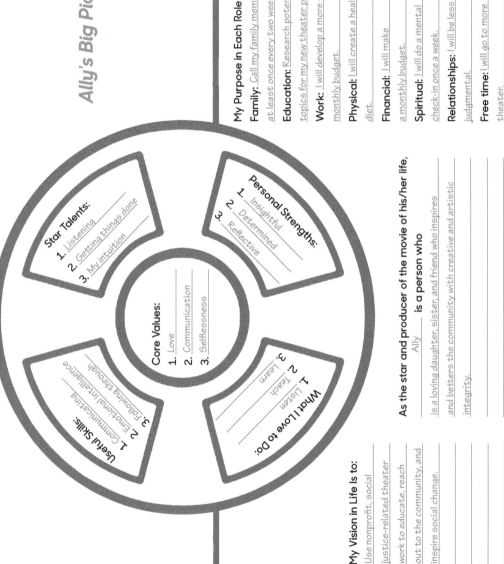

Star Talents:
1. Listening
2. Getting things done
3. My intuition

Personal Strengths:
1. Insightful
2. Determined
3. Reflective

Core Values:
1. Love
2. Communication
3. Selflessness

Useful Skills:
1. Communicating
2. Emotional intelligence
3. Following through

What I Love to Do:
1. Listen
2. Teach
3. Learn

My Vision in Life Is to: Use nonprofit, social justice-related theater work to educate, reach out to the community, and inspire social change.

As the star and producer of the movie of his/her life, _Ally_ **is a person who** is a loving daughter, sister, and friend who inspires and betters the community with creative and artistic integrity.

My Purpose in Each Role I Play:

Family: Call my family members at least once every two weeks.

Education: Research potential topics for my new theater piece.

Work: I will develop a more solid monthly budget.

Physical: I will create a healthier diet.

Financial: I will make a monthly budget.

Spiritual: I will do a mental check-in once a week.

Relationships: I will be less judgmental.

Free time: I will go to more theater.

Theme song: "Get Lucky" by Daft Punk

Tagline for the movie: "I get up every morning determined to both change the world and have one hell of a good time. Sometimes this makes planning my day difficult." —E. B. White

THIS BOOK IS ABOUT YOU, not me. But since I'm going to be your guide on a rather personal journey, I thought I should introduce myself in a preface.

Hi. I'm Dr. Christine B. Whelan. This is no ordinary self-help book, because I'm no ordinary self-help book writer. I'm an applied sociologist in the School of Human Ecology at the University of Wisconsin–Madison. I wrote my doctoral dissertation on the self-help industry. I've studied who buys self-help books, what advice is popular, and why. I've crafted rigorous content analyses of bestselling titles to uncover the formula of their success. I catalogued the advice of hundreds of guides to find the ones that had real research behind them (and the ones that were mostly made-up garbage). I've explored the assumptions, sociology, and psychology of personal improvement. And along the way, I've combed through the advice to find the nuggets of enduring wisdom in these popular paperbacks.

At the University of Wisconsin, I teach classes on purpose, meaning, and happiness. I cocreated a first-year introductory class called EcoYou: Belonging, Purpose, and the Ecology of Human Happiness, which addresses big questions like: Who am I? What is my passion and purpose? Where do I belong? How am I connected to others and to larger systems? What brings happiness and works for the greater good in human lives? I teach an upper-level class called Consuming Happiness, about all the ways we use the market economy—successfully and unsuccessfully—to increase our well-being.

I'm also a curator at the Life Reimagined Institute, a team of thought leaders devoted to helping people navigate life's transitions with purpose. Together with the best content experts from around the world, we create online and offline experiences to help real people turn their *coulda, woulda, shoulda* moments into *can, will,* and *do* successes.

Real People, Real Advice

In case you were wondering, all the stories in this book are real. The people exist. They aren't composite characters. While most folks are identified by their first name only to protect privacy, others have asked to be identified by their full, real name. The student examples quoted throughout the book are all real, too, and used with their permission.

Not only have I worked with, researched, and helped create content to help people thrive at all stages of life, I'm a big believer in practicing what I preach. I've personally completed—and benefited from—every exercise and tidbit of advice I present. The advice in this book comes from three sources: bestselling purpose-focused self-help books, academic research about purpose and meaning formation, and young-adult purpose-seekers just like you.

Indeed, that's how this book came about.

▩ THIS BOOK WORKS—AND YOUR PEERS PROVED IT

In 2011 I published *Generation WTF: From What the *^%$ to a Wise, Tenacious, and Fearless You.* It was a remix of the best of classic self-help concepts, specifically tailored to college students. I was teaching at the University of Pittsburgh at the time and had worked with hundreds of students to create and test the book. When the book was officially published, I asked a fresh batch of students to review it for me.

The first section of the book focused on the importance of getting wise—or as Aristotle would say, "knowing thyself." I presented a brief exercise on finding your purpose, asking those "why" questions and finding out what's important to you. Students told me that was the most transformative exercise in the book. "Where can we get more of these kind of exercises?" they asked.

I began to look for purpose-focused guidebooks specifically geared toward young adults. With the exception of Jon Gordon's *The Seed*; Dan Webster and Randy Gravitt's *Finding Your Way*, excellent parable-style short stories of a college student wrestling with big questions of meaning and purpose; and a few career-guidance books that briefly mentioned the importance of finding meaningful work, I came away empty-handed.

Instead, I found dozens of purpose-focused books for people in midlife. If you were having a midlife crisis or wondering what to do with the second half of your life, you could choose from a veritable library of excellent resources. So back in the summer of 2012, I set about reading dozens of these books about purpose, written for folks in their forties, fifties, and sixties. I searched for exercises that might be right or adaptable for emerging adults, questions that would be better addressed sooner rather than later in life.

Picture me in a coffee shop pondering my strengths, values, and vision. I wrote epitaphs for my tombstone. I identified my anxieties and fears. I made commitments. I reached out to mentors. I wrote my purpose statement. I'd stare off into space as I reflected—and yes, plenty of folks gave me odd looks.

To create the first draft of this book, I pulled from several dozen of the exercises that resonated most with me. I also took a deep dive into the academic literature on purpose and meaning formation, especially during the emerging-adult years. From the groundbreaking purpose research of Stanford professor Bill Damon to the academically validated scales of Carol Ryff and Michael Steger, I immersed myself in this rich world. Finally, I did interviews with real people who were living their purposes.

After my extensive reading, research, and interviews, the real fun began. In 2013 and 2014, I tested these exercises on more than three hundred students. I first gave the book to students at the University of Pittsburgh. After revising the book based on their feedback and adapting exercises for a young-adult audience, I circulated the text among a smaller group of testers at the New School, the University of Scranton, and the University of Pennsylvania. Then I ran it past a new group of University of Pittsburgh students, revised and edited the exercises even more, and by the autumn of 2014, students in my happiness class at the University of Wisconsin–Madison gave their feedback on the nearly final draft.

The advice in this book has been tested—and proved worthy—in a number of ways:

▶ It has real research to back it up.
▶ It's been tested by emerging adults like you.
▶ It's based on respected advice that's been personalized for your generation.

One of *The Big Picture* testers was Hugh, who read the book during his senior year of college. He'd started out as premed but then switched to prelaw—despite his parents' initial disapproval. "It wasn't that my parents specifically wanted to me to be premed," Hugh said, "but that they held a markedly negative opinion of lawyers and politicians."

Reading *The Big Picture* his senior year offered a welcome counterbalance to some of the uncertainty and financial insecurities that worried him as he prepared for graduation. "It helped me shed some of my more utilitarian ideas about a career path. For me, the difference between 'What career path is best suited for your skills?' and 'What career path will help you fulfill your purpose?' is very large. There are many potential answers to the first question, and fewer potential answers to the second. Reading *The Big Picture* was the first time I had ever really asked myself about my purpose, and it really did contribute to my sense of clarity and direction. My long-term goals and short-term goals didn't have to be identical."

"Today you are You, that is truer than true.
There is no one alive who is Youer than You."
—DR. SEUSS

Thinking about the concepts raised in *The Big Picture* helped Hugh settle on his career path. He reflected, "I believe I succeeded specifically because I was confident in my own unique talents. Find your strength, develop it, and don't be afraid to use it to your advantage."

This book helped Hugh and many others reach their next steps after college, so with a research-based confidence that few other improvement guides can offer, I can tell you that this book works. If you complete the exercises, you'll learn something about yourself and be better equipped to make purpose-inspired choices about your future.

I'm also confident that this book will work for *you* personally, because hundreds of your peers cowrote it. Plus, it's focused on action. Instead of just reading ideas and theories of purpose, you'll consider questions in a small-steps format to help you answer for yourself the question of purpose.

Because this book was written for emerging adults like you, it is not a preachy text about figuring out your one true purpose. You're still growing, discovering, and figuring out what's most important to you. You want to have fun, not turn everything into a future-oriented assignment. That's why *The Big Picture* focuses on the purpose *mindset*—not some singular, pressure-filled statement of purpose.

So thank you for joining me on this journey. I hope you'll give yourself the space to reflect on what's great about you, explore possibilities for the future and embrace a purpose mindset that guides you into a thriving future.

Oh, and I'd love to hear from you along the way. Reach out online at TheBigPicture.Life.

Onward!

Acknowledgments

IT IS THE FINITE NATURE OF LIFE that gives every breath meaning. This book is more than four years in the making, and loved ones who were with me at the start are now only with me in spirit. My son, Daniel Whelan Moyers; my mother, Elizabeth Murphy Whelan; and my mentor and sponsor, Lorna Jorgenson Wendt, all lived lives of great purpose, but left our earth too soon.

The work of many authors, researchers, and educators contributed to this workbook: Matt McKay, Liz Lamping, Marci Alboher, Jacqueline Herzog, Bryan Dik, Meg Jay, Kate Lombardi, Jane Walsh, Matthew Walsh, John DiIulio, Jonathan Alter, Ryan Duffy, Carol Ryff, Tatiana Boncompagni. Meredith Bazirgan, David Gould, Rebecca Pardot, Abby Wisse Schachter, Tom Anderson, Peter Scales, John Tierney, Cindy Skrzycki, and Stephanie Boddie. Regardless of the topic, I am always in debt to my academic mentors, Avner Offer and Donald Drakeman, for all my research and writing.

Susan Arellano, Trish Vergilio, and Angelina Horst at Templeton Press gave me the time to test this workbook and the purposeful encouragement to see the project through.

Maria Palermo, Chris Vereb, Greg Foley, Sam Lustgarten. Heather Baroffio, Kristie Lindblom, Kimberly Palmer, Elissa Ashwood, Brian Rokus, Fred Whelan, Jenny Heiskell, and Daniel Salmon shared personal stories with me.

Hundreds of young adults tested this book in draft form at colleges and universities nationwide. In particular, I am grateful for the detailed feedback from Megan Tierney, Hugh Hamilton, Ally Tufenkjian, Joseph Mazarella, Greta Doucette, Nico Galvan, and Natalie Shribman.

Special thanks to Julie Hudak, Emily Rowe, Jennifer Butchart, Kaitlyn Moon, Melanie DiBello and Stephanie Benincase, who worked as undergraduate researchers and data collectors for the book at various points in their college careers.

Colleagues and friends read the manuscript offered generous feedback, including Bill McGarvey, Elissa Ashwood, Naomi Riley, Christy Uffelman, Matthew Bundick, Natalia Petrzela, Christina Campolongo, Robert George, John DiIulio, Richard Klin, Jake and Rhonda Douglas, R. Shep Melnick, Tony Cernera, Kerry Cronin, Jennifer Mariano, Hitendra Wadhwa, Tim Reilly, Raul Valdez-Perez, Don Drakeman, Jeffrey Dill, Rev. Richard J. Zelik, Alexcis Lopez, and Jennifer Beaugrand.

At Life Reimagined, I have had the good fortune to find a community of thought leaders passionate about the dissemination of purpose. Special thanks to Emilio Pardo, Richard Leider, Rich Feller, Bill Thomas, Janet Taylor, Stephan Rechtschaffen, Christopher Metzler, Pamela Mitchell, John Wilson, Jeannette McClennan, Charlotte Yeh, Carey Kyler, David Eilers, Gary Bolles, and David DeCheser.

At the University of Wisconsin–Madison School of Human Ecology, I am surrounded by academics, graduate students, and administrators who are passionate about purpose. The support of Soyeon Shim, Lori DiPrete Brown, Linda Zwicker, Lynn Mecklenburg, Linda Roberts, Connie Flanagan, Roberto Rengel, Jerry O'Brien, Nancy Wong, Dee Warmath, Emily Parrott, Abra Vigna, Victoria Faust, and Dayana Kupisk has been invaluable.

Maggie Lozier, Ashley Savisky, Christina Campolongo, Darcy Hamil Scott, Lindsay Larkin, and Katrina Folberg made it possible for this mama to have time to write.

And in the tradition of saving the best for last, I thank my husband, Peter; my children Eleanor, Beatrice and John; my father, Stephen Whelan; and my parents-in-law, Katherine and John Moyers, for helping me grow into my own purpose—and share that with others.

The Big Picture

CHAPTER 1

Preproduction

THE TIME IS NOW

I always thought you just go to college and the rest figures itself out. That's what we're told. But it doesn't work like that. Going to college isn't a prescription, it's not a guide for life. No one tells you how to make it all work. Then I thought it was about setting goals, so I did that. I made one-, three-, five-, and ten-year plans. I'm a dreamer. But in one year I accomplished my two life goals—to go to Europe and graduate from college—and I had no idea what to do next. The best advice is to trust your instincts, learn about yourself, and figure out what gives you meaning and purpose. But trusting your instincts and searching for meaning is hard, especially when you feel like it's just you out there all alone. —**MARIA P.**

"**WHAT DO YOU WANT TO BE** when you grow up?"

"Where do you want to go to college?"

"What do you want to major in?"

"Do you have a job lined up after graduation?"

You've been asked some variation of these questions hundreds of times by well-meaning (but irritating) adults. Most of the how-to-be-happy advice you've been given revolves around accumulating degrees and impressive job titles. But my guess is that you know that something is missing from this conversation—that questions lurk behind these questions—and that a meaningful, happy life means connecting to something bigger.

For decades, the assumption was that those big questions weren't meant for young people. In the old way of doing things, you'd do what you had to do to get a job and make ends meet to support a family, and only after you achieved financial security could you ask what was important to you and how your gifts and talents could make a difference. Books on seeking purpose were mostly targeted at midlife adults who wanted to do something more meaningful with the second half of their lives than they did with the first.

Fortunately, times have changed. Research proves what you already know: You are at a pivotal juncture *right now*. Your personality is shaped more during your twenties than any other time in adulthood, and the experiences you have and the choices you make during these years will have a disproportionate influence on the life that you will lead. Indeed, according to psychologist Meg Jay's inspirational book, *The Defining Decade: Why Your Twenties Matter—And How to Make the Most of Them*, 80 percent of life's most significant events take place by the age of thirty-five, so to leave thoughtful consideration of these questions until a midlife crisis seems backward. Your late teens and twenties are the years when you are creating yourself in relationship to the world, and it is rightfully a time for asking big questions and formulating worthy dreams.

Just as kids effortlessly learn whatever language they hear before age five—but struggle to do so as they get older—your young-adult years are a window of opportunity to create the life you want by making conscious choices about what's meaningful to you . . . now.

Studies find that people who set and achieve goals in their twenties are more likely to report a sense of purpose, mastery, agency, and well-being in their thirties, but you don't have to lock yourself into one particular path or singular purpose for the rest of your life. Instead, research suggests that getting into a *purpose mindset*—identifying how your specific talents and values intersect with the needs of others—is the first step toward living a purposeful life.

This is the first guidebook to help young adults—high school and college students and recent grads—get into that purpose mindset. We ask questions such as:

▶ What are my talents—and how can I use those to help others and create meaning?

▶ How have my life experiences shaped who I am and what I can give?

▶ What do I value, and how can I be happy while being true to those values?

Asking and answering those questions have already transformed the lives of some of your peers: Megan read a draft of *The Big Picture* as she finished her freshman year of college and says that it gave her the perspective she needed to handle the life-changing events that unfolded next.

Megan was a serious volleyball player. In her first year of college she'd been injured twice, and as she started her sophomore year she was having differences with her coach. "After five days of tryouts," she says, "it wasn't working out—and he asked me not to come back. I was really, really upset, and I didn't know what to do with myself."

Seeking a team as well as to reclaim her identity as an athlete, Megan joined the Ultimate Frisbee club team. But during the spring semester, she collided with the biggest guy on her team and suffered a serious concussion. It wasn't her first concussion either, compounding her problems: She was unable to walk straight or sit in a room with light. She left school for several weeks as she met with neurologists to figure out what to do.

While she finished out the school year, Megan was left with permanent vertigo and severe anxiety. Contact sports were out. She started her junior year, she recalls, "without a sport and without an identity."

Looking for answers, she pulled out *The Big Picture* a second time and reread her initial responses. Megan realized that she still had much to be thankful for, and that sports weren't the only thing that gave her life purpose: "My family and friends never went away, and neither did my passion for being a teacher." The accident, and then rereading her *Big Picture* work, refocused Megan for the last two years of college.

"It was a turning point," Megan said. "Little things just don't get me fired up anymore. Little college dramas don't freak me out anymore. Now that I can see my larger purpose, I can take a step back. That's my advice to people reading this book: Look at everything that's happening around you, all the good things that are going for you, and live with a purpose mindset. If you hit a roadblock, it isn't going to end your dreams. It's all about seeing the big picture."

■ SO, WAIT. WHAT IS PURPOSE?

Megan's advice is right on target: Live with a purpose mindset. But what exactly does that mean?

Living purposefully means having a good sense of what you are trying to accomplish in your life—and an understanding of why it's important. Goals like getting into college or getting a job are just that: goals. While they are important, they are also shorter-term.

When you are in a purpose mindset, you are connecting to something that is bigger than you—and pursuing goals that are valuable and important toward achieving that end. The quest for beauty or justice isn't just about your individual desires; these bigger dreams transcend our day-to-day grind and give us the perspective we need to keep going. As writer and theologian Frederick Buechner said, you find your purpose and sense of self in the world where "the heart's deep gladness meets the world's deep hunger."

Let's be clear: Your *purpose* isn't to get into college or get a certain type of job. It isn't to marry the right kind of person or have a house in the best neighborhood. It's also probably not

A purpose mindset will

▶ Be focused on meaningful action.

▶ Have a positive impact on others.

▶ Use your talents, skills, and personal qualities.

▶ Drive your short-term life and career goals.

▶ Energize you to move forward.

about selling all your worldly possessions and becoming a missionary (although for a few that might be the path), and it's certainly not about saying no to fun.

Living purposefully isn't about glamorous work or important-sounding titles. Seemingly mundane jobs can be full of meaning when approached from a purpose mindset. So can high-profile positions that earn lots of money and things you do outside of paid work.

> This is a guide to get you thinking about the big picture, the options out there, and the hopes and dreams you have to use your time, talent, and treasure to positively influence your neighbors, your community, and perhaps even the world.

Your purpose might be fueled by faith, or it could be a secular pursuit. And since you are starting to think about these concepts at a relatively young age, your purpose will probably change over time, too.

Purpose is a key ingredient in achieving the good life, argues bestselling purpose author Richard Leider. He defines the good life as being in the right place, with the right people, doing the right work, on purpose. "Living on purpose is a choice," writes Leider in *The Power of Purpose*. "It is a way of living in which you are aware each moment of each day that you have a choice about what to say and do and how to be. Every situation presents you with a new purpose moment—an opportunity to show up on purpose—and you are conscious of the opportunities." In other words, living on purpose means becoming aware of who you are and what you are bringing to life each day as you create your good life.

I don't have a hidden agenda to steer you into a do-goody profession. In fact, short of things that are illegal or harmful to yourself or others, I don't really care what you do—as long as you are using your unique gifts to live a life that's meaningful to you.

I do, however, believe that your purpose will be bigger than just making yourself happy. Academics call this the *prosocial* nature of purpose. Prosocial behavior is

activity that benefits other people or society as a whole. If you are building friendships, helping family members, or doing something to benefit your community or
your peers, you are engaging in prosocial behavior.

Research shows that when you think about and do things for others, you are
more likely to be happy. Professors Elizabeth Dunn and Michael Norton find that
asking people to spend money on others—from giving to charity to buying gifts for
friends and family—reliably made them happier than spending that same money
on themselves.

Aristotle wouldn't be shocked by this finding. A few thousand years ago he wrote
about the difference between *hedonic* happiness—making yourself feel good by
maximizing pleasure and minimizing pain at every turn—and *eudaimonic* happiness—meaningful flourishing that comes from satisfying, other-centered work
and virtue-based action. Living purposefully falls into the eudaimonic happiness
category. While I hope you'll have many moments of pure hedonistic enjoyment on
your purpose journey, you'll also be more willing to go through some tough times
and possibly sacrifice a bit for the larger meaning behind your passions.

In his book *The Purpose Economy*, Aaron Hurst argues that this search for
eudaimonic, purposeful happiness is increasingly a necessity, not an option, for
young adults. Purpose is a verb, not a noun, he writes. It's about what we do and
how we work. "We experience purpose when we do something that's greater than
ourselves. We experience purpose when we push ourselves and grow. We experience purpose as part of a community. . . . Purpose isn't a cause, revelation, or a
luxury. Purpose is a choice."

When it comes to purpose, how are you feeling?

EXERCISE 1.1

Are You Living Purposefully Right Now?

Take a moment to answer these seven questions. Circle the number that best
corresponds to what you honestly feel right now.

I have discovered a satisfying life purpose.

1	2	3	4	5
Absolutely Untrue	Mostly Untrue	Neither True or Untrue	Mostly True	Absolutely True

I have a good sense of what makes my life meaningful.

1	2	3	4	5
Absolutely Untrue	Mostly Untrue	Neither True or Untrue	Mostly True	Absolutely True

My life has a clear sense of purpose.

1	2	3	4	5
Absolutely Untrue	Mostly Untrue	Neither True or Untrue	Mostly True	Absolutely True

I understand my life's meaning.

1	2	3	4	5
Absolutely Untrue	Mostly Untrue	Neither True or Untrue	Mostly True	Absolutely True

I enjoy making plans for the future and working to make them a reality.

1	2	3	4	5
Absolutely Untrue	Mostly Untrue	Neither True or Untrue	Mostly True	Absolutely True

I am an active person in carrying out the plans I set for myself.

1	2	3	4	5
Absolutely Untrue	Mostly Untrue	Neither True or Untrue	Mostly True	Absolutely True

Some people wander aimlessly through life, but I am not one of them.

1	2	3	4	5
Absolutely Untrue	Mostly Untrue	Neither True or Untrue	Mostly True	Absolutely True

Now, tally up your score and write it here: _____ .

This survey is a shortened combination of Michael Steger's meaning-of-life scale and Carol Ryff's purpose-in-life scale, each of which has been validated to give a pretty good idea of someone's sense of purpose. The higher your score, the more purposeful you are in how you are living your life right now. Among nearly one thousand young adults I surveyed for this research, the average score was 24 (with a possible low of 7 and a high of 35). For all the questions—and the responses—from the surveys, check out Appendix A.

Don't like your score? Many young adults are seeking more purpose, and that's great. You are also at the perfect juncture to ask these questions, so if you don't feel like you've got it all figured out, you're right on track: Only 6 percent of the young adults I surveyed could say the statement, "My life has a clear sense of purpose," was absolutely true, compared to national surveys of adults showing about 21 percent who strongly agree that their life has a clear sense of purpose.

▊ THIS BOOK WAS WRITTEN FOR YOU

Whether you dream big or are feeling a bit overwhelmed, *The Big Picture* has exercises to help you clarify what matters most to you—and help you separate what you want from the way others tell you your life should proceed.

Whether you're a go-getter with a single-minded purpose, or someone who has ideas but not a lot of commitment to any one thing in particular, *The Big Picture* will help you turn possibilities into reality.

William Damon, a psychology professor at Stanford, has spent more than a decade researching young adults and purpose. Rather than using scales and surveys, he conducted dozens of interviews and surveyed hundreds of teens and twenty-somethings for his book *The Path to Purpose*. Professor Damon finds that young adults are roughly split into four groups, each with varying degrees of purpose. Which one sounds the most like you?

▸ Disengaged. You feel like the future is out of your hands, so why bother even trying to make a difference? You're busy, sure, but it often seems like life is that empty space between panic-crazed frantic action and total boredom. If you are sick of living like this, you've come to the right place.

▶ Dreamer. You have ideas about what should happen to make the world a better place, but you haven't made any practical plans for action. If this sounds like you, you can turn these dreams into life-changing realities with the purpose-based action plan you'll find on the following pages.

▶ Dabbler. You love to start new projects, but you lose interest too quickly to turn those early action items into a purpose-based long-term plan. If this sounds like you, read on to turn your good work so far into something even more meaningful. Being present in the moment is wonderful. Setting goals and accomplishing them over time are necessary next steps.

▶ Purposeful. You've found something meaningful that you want to pursue, and you know what it takes to follow through on your goals. If this is you, I'm not surprised you've picked up this book: you know how good it feels to embrace the purpose mindset. The exercises provided here will help you take the next steps on your journey.

▒ THE CAMERA IS ROLLING

"When I look back on my life, I want to know that I did everything I could do to help others and that I didn't stand by and watch people in need. If I can determine I helped, I will have lived a fulfilling life," said Gabe, twenty, after working through the beta version of *The Big Picture*.

Gabe continued, "I believe that purpose is something that won't come at a specific moment for a person but will come when it is right in that person's life. My sense of purpose has come gradually throughout my years of college. While I believe my purpose drives my career decisions today, I still can't fully explain it to someone. *The Big Picture* helped me focus the lens. I'm still producing the documentary of my life."

Like Gabe, we are all works in progress. As we figure it out, the camera is rolling on the legacy we will leave at the end of our lives.

Some people write autobiographies to pass on their legacy. Others create scrapbooks of photos and boxes of memorabilia. In this book I challenge you to envision the documentary of your life.

Picture this: Fifty years from now you are sitting, popcorn in hand, ready to watch a movie of the story of your life. Maybe your kids and grandkids are sitting next to you. Maybe you've got a whole movie theater of friends and family watching. What film are they going to see?

The movie of your life is unfolding before you—right here, right now. While it could be a Hollywood blockbuster, odds are it's a series of home-movie clips—a video scrapbook of your legacy—to show how you used your talents and time here on Earth.

You are the producer and star of this movie, but the plot—the vision and purpose of your actions—is much bigger than you. The movie will be pretty dull if it's just about how great you are, or if all you're doing is sitting there waiting for something fun to happen as the camera rolls. Instead, this movie asks you to harness your talents, interests, and values to take action—to address problems, create solutions, and touch the lives of others so that you will inspire future generations to a life of outward-focused purpose, too.

Your purpose, then, is the thematic structure to the movie of your life. Purpose drives the plot and guides the choices you make as you work toward your vision for the world. One good way to think about purpose is that it's a commitment to do something that lights you up inside while setting the world on fire.

> *Rarely do we have wasted work, though at the time it might seem that way. We're always growing and mastering life's lessons—even hard-to-recognize ones—that move us forward on purpose.*
>
> —RICHARD LEIDER, AUTHOR

As you star in the movie of your life, you'll be asked to take on many roles—friend, student, sibling, parent, employee—and your purpose is the thread of a theme throughout all the roles you play, the things you do, and the relationships you care about most. Purpose flows from deep within you and is the center that holds, sustaining you through all the changes and phases of your life.

To live purposefully in your young-adult years doesn't mean having all the answers—or predicting how the theme of your life movie will change over time. It just means getting in the purpose mindset by grabbing the camera and starting to roll. Indeed, it's okay to shoot more footage than you will use in the final cut. There's going to be some trial and error in your efforts to figure out your purpose and how best to pursue it, just as directors leave some scenes on the cutting-room floor. Not everything you do in life will be in direct service of your purpose, but everything you do can help you better understand what purpose is and how to bring it into reality.

Movies often include an unexpected event—something happens that seems to come from nowhere—that changes the whole plot trajectory. Our lives are like that, too. As you go through *The Big Picture* and ask those questions necessary to take the next steps in the documentary of your life, I'll also challenge you to embrace John D. Krumboltz's *happenstance learning theory*: the idea that our behavior is the product of countless numbers of learning experiences resulting from planned as well as unplanned situations. Life happens. Your job is to be able to gather the skills, interests, knowledge, beliefs, preferences, sensitivities, and emotions along the way to maximize your odds of purposeful thriving.

Action movies always have that feeling of urgency; we wonder what's going to happen next. It's the same way with your purpose. Finding your purpose will help you answer the question, "What will I be when I grow up?" But that doesn't lock you into one job for life. Your purpose can encompass many careers and interests. Odds are that your purpose is bigger than all of them. The quest for purpose isn't simply about what job you should take after graduation, and it's not about what will make you happy or rich. By living your purpose, you seek to accomplish all these things, but it's not only about those superficial goals.

Of course, nothing this valuable is easy. Producing the movie of your life with intention takes time, inner searching, and outward-focused thinking. Part 1 of this book is about character development: figuring out your star qualities and the over-arching beliefs that will drive the plot forward. Part 2 challenges you to identify your vision and purpose statements—and to make commitments toward action, while part 3 helps you anticipate the plot twists along the way. From figuring out what role you want to play to the postproduction process of pulling it all together as your theme song plays in the background, this book guides you as you do the following:

Identify your star qualities.
- ▶ Discover your talents and skills.
- ▶ Realize and build on your personal strengths.
- ▶ Highlight the core values that guide your decisions.

Choose your own adventure of purpose.
- ▶ Embrace the activities you love—and how they can improve the lives of others.
- ▶ Learn why gratitude is fuel for purpose.
- ▶ Crystallize your vision of contribution.

Commit to a life of meaning.
- ▶ Learn from those whom you admire.
- ▶ Make purpose-based commitments that offer true rewards.
- ▶ See your purpose in all areas of your life.

Overcome plot twists.
- ▶ Identify your fears and anxieties—and move past these unhelpful tricks of the mind.
- ▶ Mute the peanut gallery of pressure from friends and family to do things their way.
- ▶ Make conscious choices when values collide.
- ▶ Overcome procrastination by choosing to live a life of purpose now.

 As you go through the exercises, you'll see this movie reel icon. That's a prompt to take your top answers—star talents, personal strengths, core values, vision, and purpose statement, among others—and write them in the personalized movie reel at the back of this book. I've included several copies of the reel, and

you can print out more online at TheBigPicture.Life. Once you've completed your movie reel, you'll have a one-sheet summary of the thoughtful work you've done in this book. Post it in your room, take it to your career or academic guidance counselor to guide your next meeting, and get input on it from your mentors. Share it with your close friends, too. Not only will they have insights for your next steps, they might even want to create their own Big Picture reels.

◼ FOCUS YOUR LENS

You might be holding this book for any number of reasons. Maybe your school, leadership organization, or church group has asked you to read it. Maybe your parents bought it for you. Maybe you were looking for some advice geared toward your generation about the big questions of what you've been put on Earth to do. Regardless of how the book came to you, you've been presented with an opportunity to say yes and change your life.

That's a big statement, but notice how I worded it: You have been "presented with an opportunity" to change your life. Just reading this book is one thing. Working through its exercises and committing to living a life of purpose are very different. Only you can make the choice.

In his book *Your Place in the World: Creating a Life of Vision, Purpose, and Service*, inspirational author Tom Anderson writes that finding purpose is the task of a hero. "It is through our purpose that we deliver our unique gifts into the world in ways only we can. If vision lies in the ultimate realm of all possibilities, purpose begins to answer the question, 'What is mine to do?'"

You are the hero of your life's movie. It's time for action.

CHAPTER 2

The Experiment That Could Change Your Life

■ LIVING WITH A PURPOSE MINDSET

LET'S SAY YOU WANT TO BECOME a doctor. Those MCATs didn't go too well, though, and you didn't get into medical school. Instead of stopping right there and quitting, you understand that while the *goal* was medical school, your *purpose* is healing the sick. Embracing the purpose mindset, you see that other options are available. You might work toward a *vision* of healthier children worldwide by volunteering overseas at an orphanage or pursuing a degree in public health instead. Perhaps you more deeply understand that you need to study harder and retake those MCATs. But if you mixed up your goals and purpose and thought your sole purpose was to

Jen, one of my undergraduate research assistants, likened living purposefully to being a healthy tree. At some point in your life, as you grow up, up, and up, you'll hit the point of rejection. You won't get what you want. A door you thought would be open is sealed shut. So what do you do next? If you are living purposefully, you branch out and find other ways to continue to grow. Without the purpose mindset, you're stuck.

point of rejection

get an MD degree—not the actions that follow the degree—then you're stuck when medical schools take a pass on you. There's no room to grow, and you might take a completely different course that is less fulfilling because you haven't identified the larger calling of healing.

Confusing and conflating goals and purpose—and not even thinking about the larger vision—is a common but avoidable trap for young adults. And it's no wonder: All those questions about SAT scores, college choices, and job plans are focused around specific goals of achievement. But without a vision and purpose, goals may well leave you empty. I learned that the hard way.

After college, I went to graduate school. I was there for five years, and during at least three of those years, my primary focus was writing my doctoral dissertation. Not only was this tome three hundred pages long, it was all I thought about most days. The ideas consumed me. If you'd asked me, I'd probably have told you that my purpose was to get my doctoral degree.

But then something unexpected happened: On the night that I successfully defended my dissertation—and became Dr. Christine Whelan—I cried. Okay, to be honest, I sobbed. Uncontrollably. I had accomplished what I wanted to accomplish—I had my PhD—and yet there I was, in the same room, in the same skin, in the same life. I wasn't happy, relieved, or proud: I felt alone, adrift, and depressed.

Getting my PhD wasn't my purpose, and at that moment I had no idea what my purpose *was*. I'd worked my heart out for a goal that dominated my life. I knew it was a significant milestone, an important stepping-stone along my path to purpose. But without the larger meaning, without the larger vision for the future and a sense of what was mine to do in making that future a reality, the accomplishment was meaningless.

Want to avoid being a pathetic mess of tears in a few years? Learn the difference between vision, purpose, and goals—and get into the purpose mindset now.

Vision. Your vision is your hope for the future, your dream of what could be possible. It's your call to contribute—to help others and to make the world a better place. Your vision is a problem that needs to be solved, a yearning that needs to be filled—one that calls out to you more than others. Your vision is outwardly focused, and while it's bigger than you, it's possible to accomplish or partially accomplish with passion and planning.

Purpose. Your purpose is the answer to that big question: what am I called to do? It's something about which you are passionate, and while you don't have to settle on one purpose right now, getting into a purpose mindset means identifying your personal values and how you are called to make a difference toward your vision for change.

Goals. Goals are the stepping-stones that keep you on track as you live purposefully. If we confuse long-term goals for vision or purpose, we're likely to feel empty and depressed. Achieving a goal on its own isn't particularly useful; it must have a larger meaning.

While your vision may never be fully realized, and your purpose is something you will live out for a long period of time—if not your whole life—a goal can be checked off and accomplished.

Lights, Camera, Action . . . and Meaning

Vision: Your vision is the big-picture message of the movie of your life.

Purpose: Your purpose is the thematic structure to the movie of your life. Purpose drives the plot and guides your choices.

Goals: Goals are the scenes of your life's movie.

EXERCISE 2.1

Vision vs. Purpose vs. Goals

Fill in each of the blanks with the word that fits best: vision, purpose, or goal.

1. My _____ is to get As in school.

2. My _____ is to be a voice for children in need.

3. My _____ is to be a great friend.

4. My _____ is to run a half-marathon.

5. My _____ is to make my community safe and vibrant.

6. My _____ is to use my education to educate others.

7. My _____ is to earn a million dollars in one year.

8. My _____ is democratic elections worldwide.

Answers: 1 = goal; 2 = purpose; 3 = purpose; 4 = goal; 5 = vision; 6 = purpose; 7 = goal; 8 = vision

> *You have a sacred calling. The question is, will you take the time to heed that call? Will you blaze your own path? You are the author of your own life . . . don't let others define it for you. Real power comes by doing what you are meant to be doing, and doing it well.*
> —OPRAH WINFREY, BROADCASTER AND AUTHOR

▨ PASS-I-ON: BEYOND EGO TO AN ECOYOU

When people think of living purposefully, they often, as a starting point, think of something about which they are passionate. Something they love that they would be remembered for after they die. Purpose writer Barbara Braham says that it's no coincidence that these words are linked: *Passion* contains the essence of what purpose is about:

PASS – i – ON

"Isn't that what you want to do—to make a difference in the lives of others and leave something of yourself behind—pass yourself (i) on?" she asks. We all want to make a contribution to the world, and leaving a legacy is another way of saying that you have lived a life of purpose. But, Braham points out, the *i* is not uppercase. *I* would suggest ego, and that's not what purpose is about. "Purpose is a spiritual question we live out in the material world," Braham tells us. Most important is the contribution, not who the *I* is.

Braham's clever wordplay is grounded in research. Social psychologist Jennifer Crocker draws a distinction between *ego*system motivations for our behavior—the desire to build a life around making people think good things about us, and doing the best we can to make our individual selves happy—and *eco*systems motivations for behavior, in which we prioritize the needs of others, without sacrificing our own well-being. She finds that when we act in prosocial ways by showing compassion for others, we are more likely to be happy ourselves.

By making that *i* in *pass-i-on* a lowercase letter—by focusing on our contributions, not on how our actions make us appear as individuals—we are actually more likely to feel fulfilled and *purposeful* in our life choices. Think of it as embracing an EcoYou: your purpose, your life, and your passions embedded in a web of ever-evolving interconnectedness.

■ JUST SAY YES

As you produce and direct the movie of your life, this book asks you to say yes to purposeful living. *Yes* is a very powerful word because it opens doors and allows for new adventures.

The power of saying yes is what *happenstance learning theory* is all about. John D. Krumboltz, a professor of education at Stanford University, argues that the question of what you should be when you grow up need not and should not be planned in advance. Instead, we must all learn to say yes to possibilities—happenstance—and learn from them. "Career counselors should teach their clients the importance of engaging in a variety of interesting and beneficial activities, ascertaining their reactions, remaining alert to alternative opportunities, and learning skills for succeeding in each new activity," writes Krumboltz.

It's not about making a single career decision or crafting one static purpose statement. If we learn how to explore the world and learn from that exploration, we're more likely to achieve satisfying careers and personal lives, Krumboltz's research finds.

Translation: Say yes in a purposeful way, explore, and learn from your experiences.

That's what my research assistant, Jen, learned. After reading *The Big Picture*, she concluded that embracing a purpose mindset and then rolling with happenstance learning theory was the best way to say yes to what lay ahead.

"Your life purpose isn't necessarily about finding something and sticking to it. It could be, and if that works for you, that's okay," Jen told me. "But I feel like a majority of young adults aren't ready to plan their futures because, well, the future is unplanned. How can you plan for something that is completely unplanned? That's like planning your eightieth birthday party when you're seven years old. Maybe you won't like the theme of the party anymore, or maybe you won't be in the area where you planned the party to be, or maybe you won't even be alive. There is no way of knowing, and that's okay. Not knowing isn't bad, even though our society has made the unknown scary. Not knowing can be a benefit if you let it be that way."

Toward the end of college Jen felt a lot of pressure to "figure things out," and *The Big Picture* helped her take a step back and refocus her lens to make her journey about what was personally meaningful to her. "Sometimes a career that makes bank isn't necessarily something that satisfies us. A successful doctor might not be as happy as expected. And a waitress at a restaurant could be extremely happy with her life because she enjoys what she's doing," she said.

With a laugh, Jen concluded, "Everything is up in the air. It's your life. Define happiness and purpose the way you want to. Once you take a chance, taking chances isn't scary anymore. Failure becomes less of a negative, and your life's learning process will begin."

Meg Jay, psychologist and author of *The Defining Decade*, would likely give Jen a standing ovation. Jay is a big fan of saying yes, too: Being against something is easy, she writes. What are you *for*? Saying yes to experiences means embracing a purposeful life—and weaving together a narrative of experiences that will become your story. Certainly, saying yes carries risks. But we often ignore the opportunity costs of saying no or choosing no by default, doing nothing as life passes us by.

As comedian, author, and television host Stephen Colbert said in his 2006 graduation speech to Knox College:

> Don't be afraid to be a fool. Remember, you cannot be both young and wise. Young people who pretend to be wise to the ways of the world are mostly just cynics. Cynicism masquerades as wisdom, but it is the farthest thing from it because cynics don't learn anything. Because cynicism is a self-imposed blindness, a rejection of the world because we are afraid it will hurt us or disappoint us, cynics are always saying no. But saying "yes" begins things. Saying "yes" is how things grow. Saying "yes" leads to knowledge. "Yes" is for young people. So, for as long as you have the strength to, say "yes."

Say yes when it's time to face the big questions. If that time is now, remember that *you can live a life that makes you proud, that allows you to support yourself and those you love, and that makes a difference.*

The action scenes of your movie are waiting. Say yes to producing and directing your life of meaning.

Part 1
Character Development

CHAPTER 3

Carpe Diem

IN ANY GOOD ACTION MOVIE, the opening scenes leave you with a sense of anticipation. There's been a chase, an explosion, or a quiet, tense scene that lays the groundwork for the drama to come. You have this sense that the real movie, the real action, hasn't yet begun. Then the urgency starts to build, and you think to yourself, *Here we go. Now we're headed toward something big.*

Or consider horror movies. Part of the reason we love them is the buildup. It's sort of like a roller coaster. You chug up the windy, rickety tracks. You're going slowly, clicking and climbing up and up and up. If you're a thrill-seeker, this part of the ride is a mixture of anticipation and boredom; if you're more cautious, this part is only scary because of what you anticipate is coming next.

Potential energy, as you might remember from high school physics, is stored energy. The anticipation—whether in movies, amusement park rides, or life—is the buildup of potential energy.

At that moment before a big, climactic action scene—at that moment you are perched at the top of the roller coaster—it's all potential energy. When the action begins, all that potential energy turns into kinetic energy, the energy of motion. The bigger the action, the faster the roller-coaster car moves, the more kinetic energy it has.

Right now, you are potential energy.

If you're in school or recently out, you probably feel like your real life hasn't yet begun. Yes, you are busy—taking classes, working a part-time job, volunteering, putting time and energy into extracurricular activities, feeling caught up in the drama of friendships and relationships—but somehow it all seems like a practice round for real life, which will start . . . later . . . when you're an adult. Right?

That was my line of thinking for many years. I was going to be an adult after I graduated from school, and when I had a job, a house, and a spouse. *Then* real life would begin. *Then* I'd have to take things more seriously. But now? In school? Not yet. I was on the roller coaster of life, putting in the effort just to *chug-chug-chug* up the tracks.

After college I went straight to graduate school, For another few years, I still felt like I was putting off real life. I watched my friends live *their* real lives—turning their potential energy into kinetic energy, their day-to-day decisions moving them forward—while I just hung out in school, not actually living.

So I thought.

■ STEP 1: YOU ARE CREATING YOUR OWN REALITY— RIGHT HERE, RIGHT NOW

Research has found that between the ages of seventeen and thirty, we have a distinctive way of making meaning and laying the groundwork for our futures. According to Sharon Daloz Parks, there are three steps to such meaning-making:

1. Become aware that you are creating your own reality.
2. Embark on a personal search for truth.
3. Cultivate a capacity to respond and act in ways that are satisfying to you and that you feel are just.

In my own case, I needed to take that first step. What's more, I encourage you to take it right now. Understand that you are creating your own reality and cocreating it with the world around you. You are producing and directing the movie of your own life. Wherever you are, *you are living real life right now.* What you do and say matters. The choices you make have long-term consequences. You might not feel like an adult yet, but you're making choices like one—and the consequences are certainly real enough.

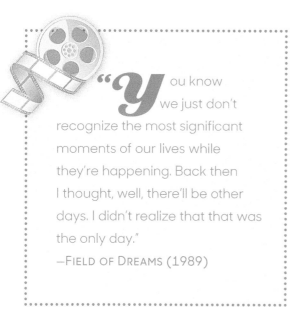

"You know we just don't recognize the most significant moments of our lives while they're happening. Back then I thought, well, there'll be other days. I didn't realize that that was the only day."

—FIELD OF DREAMS (1989)

One day in my early twenties I realized, with the force of a boulder dropping from the sky, that this *was* my real life. Two of my close friends had attempted suicide. I was immersed in big existential questions.

I came to understand that the weeks and months were passing by, and I could choose how to treat them—either as some separate and unreal time horizon or as *my real life*. I could keep screaming inside, or I could take action.

Potential is exciting when you're young. You haven't made too many mistakes, and you are being judged mostly on your plans, not your end results. People think you're great. Your parents can brag about you without your actually having done anything. Your choices seem limitless. The possibilities are endless.

But then you end up at the top of the roller coaster and you've got to make a choice: Do I just hover there on the brink, or do I put myself into motion and turn all that potential energy I've built up into kinetic energy, beginning the ride of my life?

I feel like I'm constantly stuck in a paradox. I feel like I'm not supposed to wish my life away, but I can't wait to get to "real life." How silly is that? Real life. As though the past twenty years of my life have been some sort of start-up life. I've had incredible experiences in my first twenty years, so it's dumb to think that the next twenty years will be more legitimate simply because I will have more responsibility.

Every second that you are alive is a part of real life, no matter what you're doing. Waiting for real life is a delusion we college students buy into. We are constantly told horror stories about how terrifying the "real world" can be. If we admit that we are already in the real world, then we can be held accountable for out actions and the paths we choose. Accepting the idea that they are our lives and we can do what we want with them leads to the possibility of failure and heartbreak. Why not just push it off? Because there's also a lot of joy, excitement, and good out there to do. Welcome to real life. —KAITYLN

Doing something is often scary. It means choosing a path, committing to it, and working hard to make sure you accomplish your goals. It's about hard work more than late-night musings.

Stop deluding yourself that you're just in life's preparation stage, that nothing's really happened yet, and that your choices don't matter. Not choosing is itself a choice. Not acting is definitely a choice. Remaining as potential energy means never actually *doing* anything of meaning. In some ways, it's no different from death.

We always have a mix of potential and kinetic energy going on inside of us, always doing and preparing for the next adventure. But during your late teens and early twenties, potential energy and all the excitement that comes with it seem to rule the day.

Are you ready to take the first step? Can you say, "I am creating my own reality. My real life is now," and mean it? As Buddhist monk and author Thich Nhat Hanh has written, "You have an appointment with life, an appointment that is in the here and now." Don't miss your appointment.

EXERCISE 3.1

Brainstorming for Action

After hearing, "Lights, camera . . . action!" making the next move takes courage. Jot down some notes down as you brainstorm answers to the following questions: What does it mean to you to create your own reality? What does it mean to take action? How would your life look different if you moved past the laying-the-groundwork scenes of your movie and into the action scenes that define the plot?

_____

_____

_____

_____

_____

_____

_____

_____

▪ STEP 2: EMBARKING ON YOUR PERSONAL JOURNAL OF TRUTH

Filling out college applications during my senior year in high school, I was faced with a hodgepodge of questions, including, "What is your favorite time of day?" I wasn't quite sure about the point of these short-answer queries, but I wrote, "3 a.m., when everything is clear."

You've had those late-night conversations with friends—the ones that began during middle-school sleepovers and continued through coffee- and pizza-fueled study sessions in college. You might start arguing about politics, divulging secrets, or wondering aloud about life, love, and the pursuit of happiness. It's at 3 a.m., when everything is clear and our defenses are down, that we often wrestle with deep thoughts. But in a few hours, in the light of day, we return to our busy lives and try to be more practical. All too often, we push aside the big questions.

This book is dedicated to the biggest question of all: *What am I here to do?*

My challenge to you is to ask and answer this question for yourself, in the bright light of day. "What am I here to do?" is a question of purpose, the *why* behind what you do. It's the deeper reason for the goals and motives that get you out of bed each day. Your parents and teachers probably spent a lot of time talking to you about setting goals—like getting good grades or getting into college—but my guess is that you haven't spent a lot of time really considering *why* you are here and what you are called to do with your life.

This is the second step in the three-step process that occurs between ages seventeen and thirty: embarking on your personal journey of truth.

If you've wondered what you are here to do and what the point of your life is, welcome to the human race: It's the number-one question that people of all ages want to answer. A few years back, *USA Today* asked adults what they would ask God or a Supreme Being if they could get a direct and immediate answer. The most popular question from the list they offered wasn't "Will I have life after death?" (that was number two), or "Why do bad things happen?" (That was number three) The top question adults would ask a God or Supreme Being was, "What's my purpose here?" Think about that. People are more interested in their purposes now than what will happen to them after their deaths.

If I could ask God or a Supreme Being one question
and get a direct and immediate answer, I would ask:

What is my purpose here?	39%	
Will I have life after death?	28%	
Why do bad things happen?	14%	
Is there intelligent life elsewhere?	13%	
How long will I live?	6%	

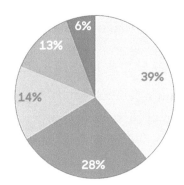

I replicated this question in a survey of nearly one thousand young adults, mostly clustered in the sixteen-to-thirty age range, and the results came out the same way.

Whether you think that purpose and meaning come from connecting to something that is bigger than you—something that transcends yourself—like God or a quest for justice or beauty, or that purpose and meaning come from pursuing goals that are valuable and important, your journey to find your purpose is an adventure to seek something intrinsically important.

A man with a why can endure any how.

—FRIEDRICH NIETZSCHE, PHILOSOPHER

Holocaust survivor, psychiatrist, and author Viktor Frankl has argued that a sense of purpose was in part what distinguished those who survived Nazi concentration camps in World War II and those who didn't. In his 1959 book, *Man's Search for Meaning*, Frankl writes that in even the most painful and dehumanized situation, life has potential meaning, and the ability to see that meaning gives you strength to keep living.

Meaning and purpose can come from religious or secular worldviews. A life devoted to the purpose of feeding the hungry can come from a desire to serve the glory of God and his people or from a belief in the intrinsic worth of the one and only life we are given. Faith in a higher power can guide a life of generosity, sacrifice, and good work, as can faith in humanity. It doesn't have to be religious—but it must be bigger than you are.

"To be human is to dwell in faith, to dwell in the sense one makes out of life— what seems ultimately true and dependable about self, worth, and cosmos, whether this is in secular or religious terms," writes Sharon Daloz Parks in her book *Big Questions, Worthy Dreams*, about the search for meaning in young-adult years.

The following chapters of this book will help you make sense of what seems true and dependable about yourself and what kinds of acts seem to have worth and meaning for you. But let's start with the cosmos: the biggest questions about faith.

EXERCISE 3.2

The Biggest Questions of All

Take a few minutes to think about your worldview. Some religions would think of this as a profession of faith in which you state your core beliefs, but yours doesn't have to be tied to one religion or any religion at all. Be open to borrowing from any tradition or philosophy. There are no right answers. Indeed, according to my survey of young adults, high-purpose folks are equally likely to be religious or nonreligious.

Write down your responses to the following questions:

❋ *Do you believe in God or a higher power? If so, how much does this belief influence your life and decisions?*

❋ *Do you believe that we are all part of the energy of the universe, part of the ebb and flow of creation? If so, how much does this belief influence your life decisions?*

❋ *Where does your strength, energy, and passion come from?*

❋ *Is your life (and, by definition, your purpose) preordained by a Supreme Being, or do you have free will to choose and change the path and purpose of your time here on Earth?*

_____

_____

_____

_____

_____

_____

This is big, heavy stuff, so if you don't have too many coherent answers, don't worry. No one has these answers, at least not at first. The idea is just to get you thinking about *your beliefs* as an individual. Your parents may have a different worldview, and that's okay. If you do this exercise in a group, you will probably end up with many varied answers. Even pastors and theologians will tell you that your profession of faith is likely to change over the course of your lifetime; theirs do as well.

For Maria, one of the earliest testers of and inspirations for my writing *The Big Picture*, embracing a purpose mindset allowed her to thrive, despite some very rocky years. Now, at twenty-seven, Maria says her purpose is to use photography to improve the lives of others. In addition to shooting weddings on weekends, Maria takes portraits of individuals and families and teaches a photography class on Sundays, donating the proceeds from both of these jobs to the Cystic Fibrosis Foundation. "It's nice to use your talents just to help people," she says. "I'm giving up one Sunday afternoon a month to help raise money so that drugs can come to the market that save lives. My loans will be there, but this is a way I can use my gifts to really make a difference."

Notice that Maria didn't mention religion once, but her values would be at home in any of the world's faiths. Maria's faith is in humanity and in herself, she says. As the first person in her family to attend college, she received no financial help and no mentoring for the road ahead. She was admitted to her dream school, but when the promised financial aid didn't materialize, she had to withdraw after a year—with $15,000 in debt just to make it that far.

"For two and a half years I worked at Starbucks, at a hotel, at a restaurant, got my real estate license, and worked as a lifeguard, trying to figure out what to do. I moved back home, retook the SATs, and read a bunch of books to try to figure things out. I read *What Color Is Your Parachute?*, *Who Moved My Cheese?*, and took Myers Briggs tests. I pursued any avenue I could think of, but none of that advice seemed like it was relevant for me where I was in my life," Maria says. "What I really needed was *The Big Picture*," she laughed, "but you hadn't written it yet!"

One day at the pool where she was working as a lifeguard, Maria met a photographer who agreed—after much cajoling—to let her accompany him on a shoot. Soon she was hooked, again.

"I had rolls and rolls of film from middle school on, but I didn't have a mentor to help me realize that this could be a career. I would love to teach photography as a vocation for young kids. There are so many programs for sports—learning boxing as a way to stay off the streets and not do drugs, that sort of thing—but what about artistic kids? I'd love to be the mentor I never had."

After a few more false starts, Maria was able to return to school and complete her degree, where she majored in politics. She interned in the city council's office and took a low-paid position there after graduation. Things were so financially strapped that she applied for food stamps and welfare to try to make ends meet—paying more than $1,000 monthly in college loans left little room for rent and food—but she didn't qualify because the aid rubric didn't take her loans into consideration.

In need of cash and hoping to "bring the creative back" into her life, she decided to take a leap back into wedding photography. "I offered to shoot a wedding for free on Craigslist. No one took me up on that, but I did get several other jobs, which eventually led to weddings," she says. The first year she photographed two weddings, the next year it was five, and for the last two years she's had twenty-five weddings to keep her busy. While she's kept a day job, it's photography where she feels the most purposeful.

"It's really about the people. I don't need it to be about the money," she says of photography, "and I've gotten it so that I'm okay each month. I can pay my bills, and that allows me to give the gift of photography as much as I possibly can."

This is where her faith in humanity—and her call to the service of others—guides her life. In addition to raising thousands of dollars for the Cystic Fibrosis Foundation, Maria volunteers for meaningful work wherever she can find it.

"Through friends of friends, I heard about a couple who were high school sweethearts. They got engaged and then the guy went off to Afghanistan and sustained a brain injury while serving our country. He was coming home and had six weeks to live. They wanted to get married before he died. They were throwing together a wedding at the last minute and had no money. They posted on Craigslist and

Facebook for donations. When I heard about this, I offered to take the photographs for their wedding. I would have gone to clean plates off the table, it didn't matter. I wanted to help. I took those wedding photos, and two weeks later he died," she says. "That family will treasure those photos forever, and I feel blessed and grateful that I could do that for them.

"My faith really is in myself and my ability to live my values," Maria says. "My goal is to never pervert photography. If it's just business, that's not the point. I want to be serious and to be taken seriously. If what you do is a passion, you should treat it in a way that's respectful."

While Maria wishes she'd had some mentors who had encouraged her to pursue photography earlier, she acknowledges the maturity and trust in herself that she's gained from the harder path. "I could do a regimented job of any sort, I think, if it had purpose for me. The fulfillment I get from teaching people and working with people is what I love. I can't be a doctor, but I can still be helpful to people in need by using my own gifts and living my purpose."

Live Life and Be Happy

We all are born into this life, and I believe that it must be lived well. There's a quote that motivates me: "And in the end, it's not the years in your life that count. It's the life in your years." I believe in packing as much as I can into the years that I have—more importantly, making a difference along the way. —SAM

The Pursuit of Happiness?

Maria is living a life of meaning and purpose—and she'd tell you that she is happy. Aristotle would say she is finding eudaimonic happiness. Fun isn't the end goal, and yet there's a lot of joy and laughter—and yes, fun—mixed in along the way.

Like you, Maria still faces challenges—and she is just barely making enough money to make ends meet. But she's meeting the future with enthusiasm and hope.

In the last few decades, psychology has given a lot of attention to the study of happiness and well-being. In a nutshell, research has found that the things we think will make us happy—money, stuff, new relationships, different environments—actually do little to affect our happiness. The tough stuff we do in pursuit of a purposeful life is what's necessary to have good mental health down the line.

"*I*s there some predetermined plan driving all the decisions that we make, or are we ourselves making our choices based on our own free wills? These mental thoughts, our liminal phase. Childhood is about magic, but teen is about mystery. It is a time when the world suddenly gets closer and colors seem brighter. Rules seem ready to be broken. Y'all may have different problems, but it is the same problem. You've got to figure out what you want."
—REMEMBER THE DAZE (2007)

Why? Because there are different kinds of happiness, research finds. There's happiness that's about pleasure and happiness that's about meaning. While new toys and fun experiences can bring us pleasure, it's personal purpose in the service of a larger vision that brings long-term satisfaction. That's why when psychologists talk about good mental health, it's usually defined to include benefits that give a person the feeling that there is purpose in and meaning to life. To be a mature person, then, means having a clear understanding of life's purpose, a sense of directedness, and intentionality.

Put another way, buying that new iPad may make you happy for the next hour

(How fun is it to open up the pretty white package and take out that brand-new, superpowerful toy?), but it will not give you a sense of long-term psychological well-being. What about volunteering at an organization that trains teenagers to help the elderly in the community use an iPad, so that they can keep in touch with their families and FaceTime with their grandkids? Or perhaps designing a new app for the iPad that will bring a smile, teach a skill, or help people stay organized? That kind of iPad fun can give you long-term satisfaction rather than a fleeting sense of enjoyment.

As I show in the following chapters, living purposefully means finding the realm where doing what you love—doing what makes you happy, what comes naturally to you, the kinds of things that make you excited and lose track of time—meets a need that is greater than your own individual pleasure.

STEP 3: JUST AND SATISFYING ACTION

To live a meaningful life, you've got to know who you are. Most of us haven't spent a lot of time doing the proactive inner searching to figure out who we are, both within ourselves and as distinct from others.

When you were a tiny baby, you didn't know that you were separate from your mother or caregiver. Indeed, you thought that you were an appendage of that person—like an arm or a leg—and connected to them. It took you a year or so to learn that you were indeed a separate person. Even as adults we don't always separate our opinions from those of others and we often confuse what others think we *should* do with what we *want* to do.

Have you ever purchased a pair of jeans that you wanted to fit, but just don't? They are the right brand, the right style, and they looked so cool at the store—but when you get them home, you look in the mirror and realize that they are too small, too big, or just hang weird.

Often, we make the right choice, but for the wrong person. We choose what we should do for the person we hoped or believed we were, rather than the person we really are. If it's just a pair of jeans, you can be disappointed and frustrated, but you can return them fairly easily. If it's a decision about a job or a romantic partner, the process isn't so simple.

Some of us assume that our schooling helps us make wise choices. Before sending us out into the world to deal with jobs, relationships, and everyday life, our high school and college courses, guidance counselors, and advisors work through a series of these types of questions with us:

- ▸ What are my talents and skills?
- ▸ What kinds of activities do I enjoy, and which ones might be useful in paid or volunteer capacities?
- ▸ What are my core values?

Wait. . . . No? You didn't graduate from high school with answers to these questions? Well, you are not alone.

Nicholas Lore writes in *Now What? The Young Person's Guide to Choosing the Perfect Career,*

> People who raise puppies for search and rescue, as guide dogs for the blind, and other demanding doggy professions put puppies through a series of eleven puppy aptitude tests that sort out which dogs excel at those functions and which would make better family pets. . . . I find this a troubling question: Which group offers more guidance for the youngsters they are supposedly helping train and educate to succeed, colleges or dog breeders?"

Whether you think of this book as puppy-training school or a deep thoughts guide, any way you cut it, to cultivate a capacity to live a satisfying life that has meaning, you've got to research yourself and learn how you are unique and separate from others. The research need not entail hours of navel gazing, but you can still learn enough about yourself to make lasting commitments to meaningful pursuits and relationships that will allow you to thrive.

Your talents and skills are different from those of your friends. The activities you enjoy may not be the ones that your parents hoped you'd enjoy when they created that busy schedule for you as a kid. The core values that guide your life may be different from those of your priest. While many people shape us into who we are, before we can make commitments to live a life of purpose—and take steps to produce and direct the individual movie of our calling—we need to understand what makes us tick. That's the work ahead.

"Everything has a purpose, even machines. Clocks tell the time, and trains take you places. They do what they're meant to do. . . . Maybe that's why broken machines make me so sad; they can't do what they're meant to do. Maybe it's the same with people. If you lose your purpose, it's like you're broken. . . . Right after my father died, I'd come up here a lot. I'd imagine the whole world as one big machine. Machines never come with any extra parts, you know. They always come with the exact amount they need. So I figured if the entire world was one big machine, I couldn't be an extra part. I had to be here for some reason. And that means that you have to be here for some reason, too."
—HUGO (2011)

CHAPTER 4

Identify Your Talents, Strengths, and Skills

VERONICA IS AN ORTHOPEDIC SURGEON who specializes in conditions of the shoulder, elbow, and hand. She was completing her final fellowship in 2010 when a devastating earthquake in Haiti killed more than two hundred thousand people and injured untold thousands more. "We've seen natural disasters or manmade disasters that occur all the time, but I was compelled to go immediately because I knew there were going to be extremity crush injuries, which lead to gangrene, septic shock, and death," Veronica explained.

For three days, Veronica amputated limbs and saved lives in tents with rudimentary medical supplies. "I'm glad I went, and I think I saved lives. The whole thing was surreal. All of the concepts that make up modern medicine—the patient's bill of rights, confidentiality, informed consent—all of those things just fell by the wayside, and it was like a war zone.

"But that was three days of my life. Yes, the impact was hopefully big, and it was a meaningful experience, but that's not what I think of when I think about living purposefully. It's what you do every day, not once in a while," she said.

Being a surgeon is a perfect match for Veronica's talents and personality, but in college, she wasn't a premed major. After briefly considering management consulting, she took a year off and went to San Francisco to work at a molecular biology lab, "But I was totally checked out," she admitted. "Part of it was immaturity, but part of it was that the pace wasn't well suited to my personality. I realized that I loved action."

In medical school, Veronica liked all her rotations, but she found that when she worked with the orthopedic surgeons, the hours flew by. "When you are a hand surgeon, you are really, really specialized, but you are treating a vast and broad patient population—from fourteen months old to ninety-six years old, men and women, people on dialysis and professional athletes. I felt like it would maintain my interest forever."

After ten years of school and fellowships, Veronica now runs her own practice in Florida. She is living purposefully, and she is very successful. She sees living her purpose as a day-to-day activity. "I do get to make a lot of money doing what I love, but it also allows me to take on charity cases. If you are a child and you are unfunded, I will help you. I decided right off the bat that if a kid came into my office, it didn't matter if his parents could pay. They were going to get care. It's not like I have my own charity or do it through a nonprofit. It's just a decision that I make that I uphold day to day," Veronica says. "Most pediatricians know that about me now. I didn't have to publicize it. Sometimes the most important impact is the one that goes unnoticed."

With a top-flight education and a nearly unstoppable will, Veronica's parents and friends always imagined she'd be an academic doctor or work at a big-name, prestigious hospital. Instead, she runs a private practice in a small suburb. "I've taken people by surprise because I realized that what was more important to me was to earn an impeccable reputation in the area I service, rather than national recognition," she said.

"I love seeing patients. I pride myself on the fact that I try to make my practice a little more personable, a little more accessible than surgeons have historically been. The more things that I can control, the fewer mistakes are made, and the better the patient does. This is what I'm good at. I'm playing to my strengths and using my skills in a way that can make a difference."

✳ ✳ ✳

If we were watching the movie of Veronica's life, the opening scenes might show her as she identified her talents, strengths, and skills. We'd see clips of her struggling to figure out the next steps in her career and watch her combine her love of interacting with people, healing, and working fast-paced action into a fulfilling career in medicine that lets her live out her commitment to helping children in need.

In this chapter I ask you to look inward to identify the talents, skills, and strengths that are your personal gift to the world. These character traits are what make you the star of this meaningful life documentary. While your talents, skills, and strengths overlap, I provide a variety of exercises so that you can choose which are the most helpful in your personal journey.

■ RECOGNIZING YOUR TALENTS

Adele is not athletic. Someone once said that watching her run was like seeing a baby giraffe in action—limbs flailing everywhere. Sports aren't her thing, and yet when she steps on a golf course she swings with grace and makes perfect contact nearly every time.

Tony is an extrovert. He thinks nothing of striking up a conversation with strangers or speaking in front of large groups of people. While public speaking ranks among many people's top fears, Tony is at ease in or in front of a crowd.

Emily likes solving puzzles. Riddles, Rubik's Cubes, and brainteasers are mental play for her. Some are more challenging than others, but she loses herself as she focuses on untying the knot and cracking the code.

Your talents are things that seem to come naturally to you. They are the things that other people think are hard but you find easy. On a tennis court Adele would be ducking for cover. Ask Tony to solve a puzzle, and he'll want to tear his hair out. And both Emily and Adele cower in fear at the thought of speaking in front of a crowd.

Talents are different from skills, acquired knowledge, and interests. You can learn new things, and your interests will change over the course of your life, but your talents will stay with you for the long haul. While it's hard to create talents that aren't there at this point, you can build on your existing talents and hone your skills to meet the goals you set down the line.

So what seems like it comes naturally to you? Are you a talker? Are you the hub of all news and information for your set of friends? Does a math lecture go by in a blink while English Lit seems to drone on and on? Do you have an eye for fashion? Do you gather lots of information before making a decision, or do you follow your gut? Do you have a great memory? Are you at ease with abstract concepts?

As Cori filled out Exercise 4.1, she noted that having a positive attitude in almost every situation was something that she did effortlessly. "I love having fun and not taking life and its mistakes too seriously, and I find that I can effortlessly put a positive spin on even the most negative situations." When Jordyne pondered her role in a group, she found her place as a supporter. "I am not a slacker, but I am not the most bold (the leader) of the group. However, I will step up to be the leader if no one else takes charge," she wrote. At work, Xin said she enjoyed "having a conversation with people about their inner feelings, and trying to give people comfort solving little problems."

This exercise is very you-based. It's inward-focused, because without basic self-awareness, it's hard to know where you'll be called to serve and how best to use your talents to make a difference in the world. Your generation is accused of being narcissistic and egotistical; ironically, creating a talent list is challenging for most people.

Your Star Qualities

Talents: Your talents are things that seem to come naturally to you. They are the things that other people think are hard, but you find easy.

Strengths: The qualities that make you a great character and allow you to shine in difficult situations.

Skills: Something you've learned to do—a competence that is the result of your experiences, education, and training.

EXERCISE 4.1

Identify Your Talents

Look at the definition of talents on page 46, and ask yourself, "What comes naturally to me?" To help you answer this question, follow the prompts below. As you reflect, there's no need to overthink your answers. If you chuckle as you're writing, smile, or have fond memories, you're on the right track.

I'm most myself when I'm

_____

_____

What I do effortlessly is

_____

_____

In my free time, I enjoy

_____

_____

If I'm working with a group, I usually fill the role of the (expert, supporter, organizer, etc.)

_____

_____

My favorite sports/hobbies are:

_____

_____

In school, these classes are easy for me:

_____

_____

At work, I enjoy doing these tasks:

_____

_____

While some people might think these things are boring or difficult, I find them interesting and easy most of the time:

_____

_____

People praise me for

_____

_____

When I'm asked to solve a problem, I

_____

_____

If you're still stuck, some of the talents on the following list might jump out at you as ones you possess. But as with all lists, be sure you're selecting talents that you really have—ones that truly come easily to you—*not* ones you hope to have or think you should have.

Abstract thinking	Great sense of smell	Remembering ideas
Artistic abilities	Hand-eye coordination (from video games to sports)	Remembering numbers
Athletic abilities		Remembering people's faces
Being persistent	Having a positive attitude	Researching, then acting
Concrete thinking		
Critical thinking	Leading others	Supporting others
An eye for bargains	Logical thinking	Understanding my own moods and their causes
An eye for detail	Making people laugh	
Fashion sense	Organizing myself and others	Working with others
Following my gut		
Great hearing	Reading people and understanding their moods	

By identifying your talents, you're highlighting a building block for future action—and taking a big step toward living a purposeful life. For Erika, the list above helped her note her abilities: organizing herself and helping others get organized, supporting others, researching and then acting, concrete thinking, and logical thinking. As she reviewed all her talents, she concluded that her top talents were "being able to plan and then act, thinking about concrete ideas, thinking logically, helping others to improve themselves, listening carefully to others' thoughts and feelings, and supporting others when they are in need by listening or acting to help them."

EXERCISE 4.1 (CONTINUED)

Identify Your Talents

Review everything you've written in the exercise and noted in the box. Now write down your talents.

My talents are . . .

_____

_____

_____

_____

 Of these talents, which are your top three? Write them down in your movie reel in Appendix B.

Most Commonly Listed Talents

- ▶ Making people laugh
- ▶ Leading others
- ▶ Supporting others
- ▶ Remembering faces

- ▶ Researching, then acting
- ▶ Logical thinking
- ▶ Being persistent
- ▶ Thinking of others' feelings

IDENTIFY YOUR STRENGTHS

Brian is a producer at a major news network, and he would say that journalism is his calling: "My purpose is to do justice to the amazing stories that I've been privileged to tell." His talents and personal strengths make him an excellent fit for that calling.

> Television is very collaborative. You have to be a team player. There are also specific skills or talents you need, such as being a good writer. But there's one overarching quality that's probably the most important: Being a nice and low-key person.
>
> Granted, that seems pretty obvious. But in my job, I need to deal with coworkers I know well and complete strangers. Sometimes I'm trying to convince those strangers to share—for the first time—incredibly personal and painful stories in front of a TV camera and lights. Other times, I'm asking for access to a place or for information that might not necessarily be in that person's interest for me to have. I've defused situations with police or security upset about us shooting a specific location. In nearly every case, I've found the way to get what you want (and to get your job done) is to be nice and as nonconfrontational as possible. I've been in the field with other producers who take the opposite approach, and while being contrite might not be the most emotionally satisfying approach in the moment, it will help you accomplish your goals.
>
> A general flexibility is essential in what I do. "It is what it is" is one of my favorite sayings. It applies to things both big and small: A character you were counting on for your story suddenly pulls out? It is what it is. You need to scuttle your personal plans for the weekend because you're hopping on the next plane to wherever for breaking news? It is what it is. I'm not saying that you don't try fix a problematic situation. But when the point comes that you know it's not going to happen, I don't spend time I

don't have freaking about it. You accept it and move on. In most cases, I'll have some kind of plan B, which makes moving on a lot easier.

I also try to find humor in everything. For some stories we cover, it might be dark humor, but it's humor nonetheless. When things get so bad that you can only laugh . . . then laugh.

Brian's talents and personal strengths make him a great television producer. They also make him a fascinating person to talk to. What are your strengths, the characteristics that would make a friend love you and an employer hire you? Being able to identify your best qualities is a life skill that will serve you well beyond those five-hundred-word college essays. Exercise 4.2 can help you pinpoint your strengths.

Ask a friend

What talents and strengths have you nurtured and encouraged in yourself over the last few years? What talents and strengths have been on the back burner? Have you buried any of your talents and strengths because your parents or teachers didn't praise you for them—or encouraged you to follow a different path?

Ask a friend or a sibling, someone who has known you for a long time, "What are my top talents and strengths?" Compare their list with yours. Have you embraced those talents or strengths that they mentioned? If not, why not? Have you tried to avoid a particular talent or strength? If so, why?

EXERCISE 4.2

Strengths Search List

So, what are your strengths? The below list is adapted from Carol Adrienne's *The Purpose of Your Life*, with many additions from the hundreds of testers who contributed to this book. It's certainly not comprehensive, but it should prompt you to begin thinking about what makes you *you*.

Go through the list and check the words that seem like they are qualities you possess. Then challenge yourself by adding a few of your own.

☐ Adventurous	☐ Generous	☐ Patient
☐ Brave	☐ Gentle	☐ Persuasive
☐ Calm	☐ Genuine	☐ Playful
☐ Comforting	☐ Humble	☐ Practical
☐ Compassionate	☐ Humorous	☐ Quick-thinking
☐ Confident	☐ Insightful	☐ Reflective
☐ Courageous	☐ Inspiring	☐ Romantic
☐ Creative	☐ Intelligent	☐ Spontaneous
☐ Determined	☐ Joyful	☐ Strong
☐ Direct	☐ Kind	☐ Supportive
☐ Energetic	☐ Knowledgeable	☐ Tolerant
☐ Entertaining	☐ Loving	☐ Trustworthy
☐ Enthusiastic	☐ Nonjudgmental	☐ Visionary
☐ Fair	☐ Open	☐ Wise
☐ Faith-filled	☐ Optimistic	☐ Witty
☐ Flexible	☐ Original	

Additional strengths that I possess:

_____   _____   _____

_____   _____   _____

To go a little deeper, think about specific situations in which your strengths shone through. This exercise can be especially useful if you are preparing for a job interview, because potential employers love to ask a variation on the question, "Tell us about a time where you faced a challenge and how you handled it."

In their book *Make Your Job a Calling*, Bryan Dik and Ryan Duffy, psychologists who study meaning-making in careers, find that a good understanding of personal strengths is useful for acing job interviews, but it's also key to choosing a career path that can be a lifelong calling.

For example, as Matthew thought of his personal strengths, he remembered an experience from his time volunteering for the Wounded Warrior Project. He met a service member who was struggling to adapt to civilian life—and life with a disability. Since Matthew's own brother had been wounded in service, Matthew was able to talk to this young man for hours. "We discussed his tours in Iraq, the horrible things he had seen and done, alcoholism after his medical retirement, and dealing with a baby on the way," remembers Matthew. Then together they devised a plan of action to have him be reassessed and paired up with the medical and psychological help he needed to heal. "Today, that man is working with a New York senator. He has a three-year-old baby boy and a girl on the way. He's been doing well after his reevaluation and transfer to new doctors and counseling professionals," reported Matthew with pride.

Looking back on the challenging situation, Matthew recognized his ability to identify the problem and work through thorny personal issues so that this service member could get the help he needed. Matthew identified his own openness to discussion, ability to be vulnerable when talking about personal experience, and ability to set clear goals as the personal strengths that helped him succeed.

Career coaches ask their clients to think of a situation in which they were at their best and answer a series of questions to get a list of personal strengths, just as Matthew did. Exercise 4.3 takes you through this same process.

EXERCISE 4.3

The Interview

Think of a situation in which you were at your best. It can be in any area of your life: perhaps a shining moment at work, a difficult situation in your family or personal life that you overcame, or a volunteer moment where you excelled and felt great about your accomplishments. The key is to *think of a time when you were challenged and you came through quite successfully.*

Using a step-by-step account, how did the situation unfold?

_____

_____

_____

What did you do well?

_____

_____

_____

What was the outcome?

_____

_____

_____

Thinking back on it, what specific personal strengths did you show in this situation? List as many as you can.

_____   _____

_____   _____

_____   _____

_____   _____

Now put a check mark next to what you would consider your five top strengths. List them on the five lines provided below for Personal Strength. In what other situations have you observed those strengths?

Personal Strength 1

_____

I also used this strength when . . .

_____

_____

_____

Personal Strength 2

_____

I also used this strength when . . .

_____

_____

_____

Personal Strength 3

_____

I also used this strength when . . .

_____

_____

_____

Personal Strength 4

_____

I also used this strength when . . .

_____

_____

_____

Personal Strength 5

_____

I also used this strength when . . .

_____

_____

_____

Commonly Noted Personal Strengths

▸ Quick thinking

▸ Compassion

▸ Strong work ethic

▸ Planning

▸ Relating to others

Strengths in Action

In ninth grade at my first high school swim meet, I had to swim the 500 free (twenty laps in a row) for the first time. I was so nervous and on the verge of tears when my best friend got put in it as well. She was more nervous and upset than I was, so I put all of my feelings aside to comfort and encourage her. By doing this, I allowed myself to calm down and swim the best 500 of the season. —ALLISON

Look over all of your strengths. What are your top three? Write these down in your movie reel in Appendix B.

▮ IDENTIFY YOUR SKILLS

Jenny started working as a barista at a local Pittsburgh coffee shop when she was nineteen. She served up lattes and cappuccinos throughout college, and when she graduated she took a job at a nonprofit. But a desk job just wasn't the right fit, and after a few years she wanted a change.

"During those years working as a barista, I loved my coworkers. I realized I loved waiting on people and hearing stories about them. You tried to remember everyone's orders. There was so much energy," she said. "I realized I missed that."

When the coffee shop expanded to a new location, Jenny took a job there as a store manager. "I like building a team and watching the team create their own dynamic. To see people snap into formation on a Saturday is amazing. I like working with the customers, and I'm a problem-solver." At twenty-seven, Jenny now manages the largest of the company's branches; she's calm and in charge of a bustling shop with dozens of employees taking shifts from 6 a.m. until midnight.

※ ※ ※

A skill is something you've learned to do—a competency that is the result of your experiences, education, and training. Skills are among the gifts that will help you live out your purpose; skills also will relate directly to jobs you'll have. You possess many skills, even if none are popping to mind right now. Some are so basic that they won't make a top-five list of your greatest skills (like the fact that you can read and write), while others are important assets that you may not have fully identified.

As mentioned earlier, there will be some overlap between your talents, strengths, and skills, and that's a good thing. For Jenny, her talent for group dynamics and a personality that thrives on business has led her to hone her skills as manager of a busy coffee shop.

Adele's talent for golf led her to join her school's team, where she learned the skills she needed to become a near-scratch golfer. Emily's talent for cracking the code of puzzles led her to a career in the biological sciences, where she became skilled at uncovering natural mysteries. Tony used his extroverted personality and love of an audience to get involved in student government, give campaign speeches, and improve his skills as an orator.

If you have a talent for communicating, you might have spent some time improving your writing and public-speaking skills. If you have a talent for figuring out how things work, you might have honed your skills at car maintenance or website development.

Of course, just because you are skilled at something doesn't necessarily mean it is one of your natural talents. We often have to learn things and get out of our comfort zones to succeed—and those skills are very valuable, even if they aren't core talents. For example, personal finance may not be your strong suit, but after learning the ins and outs of your college-loan package and spending hours on the phone negotiating a better deal, you feel pretty skilled in the how-tos of paying for school. It's going to be up to you to decide whether something is a *skill* or a *talent*.

On page 61 is a small sampling of skills you might possess, broken down—as Richard Bolles does in *What Color Is My Parachute?*—into types of skills. There are plenty of other skills you might write down for yourself. This list is just to give you a nudge in the right direction.

EXERCISE 4.4

Identify Your Skills

Skills with Things	Skills with Information	Skills with Others	Internal Skills
Athletics	Analyzing	Advising	Big-picture thinking
Biking	Budgeting	Coaching	Dressing well
Carpentry	Creating content	Communicating	Emotional intelligence
Cleaning	Decorating	Connecting people	Exercising regularly
Computing	Designing	Delegating	Following through
Cooking	Giving presentations	Entertaining	Goal-setting
Crafts	Inventing	Evaluating others	Imagination
Growing things	Managing information	Helping others	Initiating
Hiking	Observing	Leadership	Learning
Music	Organizing	Managing	Physical strength
Painting	Planning	Motivating	Positive thinking
Reading	Problem solving	Negotiating	Relaxing
Repairing	Researching	Performing	Risk-taking
Surfing the Web	Shopping	Persuading	
Using my hands	Translating	Raising children	
Using tools	Visualizing	Selling	
	Working with numbers	Teaching	
	Writing		

Brainstorm on your skills and describe them here:

_____

_____

_____

As you brainstorm about your various skills, one might pop into your head that gives you pause—a skill that you *can* do, but one that you don't usually *want* to do. For example, while you can walk a dog, it might not be something you want to do twice a day, every day—or forever.

Disregard the can-do skills and focus on the *want-to skills*, the ones that you could see yourself using every day without getting bored or going crazy. Skills that you have but don't enjoy using can be helpful, but you're not going to want them to be a major part of living purposefully if you can avoid it. For example, you may have grown up knowing how to trim hedges, but you don't necessarily want to be a landscaper.

Brainstorm: Boost Your Skills

What skills do you admire in other people that you think can be helpful—and attainable—for you?

▶ Brainstorm on your own: Who do you admire? Why? What skills do they possess?

▶ Brainstorm with a group: After each of you share the skills that you admire in other people, ask what's good, useful, or meaningful about that skill set. Is it reasonable for you to try to attain those skills?

You might also come across skills you have that suck the life right out of you. In their book, *Live Your Calling*, Kevin and Kay Marie Brennfleck call these "killer skills." You might be really good at these can-do skills, but you want to use them sparingly. For example, if you can negotiate a hard bargain but you're drained at the end of the session, this might be a killer skill. While it's good to know that you have such skills, for the purposes of our work in this book, they aren't going to be fulfilling.

Star skills are skills you have that you enjoy. Exercise 4.5 gives you space to list your star skills.

My star skills are working with other people, especially children, being a creative leader and facilitating and managing groups, evaluating and motivating others, organizing and planning, being active and athletic (including hiking and biking). I also consider creating things, being imaginative, and artistic to be a star skill. —CORI

EXERCISE 4.5

Your Star Skills

My star skills are . . .

_____

_____

Of these, which are your top three star skills? Write these down in your movie reel in Appendix B.

With this chapter, by putting your lists of talents, strengths, and skills into one place, you've begun to fill out your movie reel. As chapters go on, you can see what types of patterns emerge.

CHAPTER 5

Lose the Shoulds, Find the Values

IN HIGH SCHOOL, HEATHER HAD NO IDEA how her diverse interests could turn into a career. "I thought I wanted to be a dolphin trainer because I liked to swim. I thought about journalism, too, but I wasn't interested in those classes. I'd done some vocational tech drafting and design, and while I sort of enjoyed that, it wasn't exactly my thing, either. I checked the liberal arts box when I applied to college because I didn't know what I wanted to do," she said.

"One day I asked my mom how she knew she should be a hairdresser, and she said that she was good at it. But that answer didn't help me much. So all my friends were going away to college, and I didn't know what to do. My first year of an associate degree program didn't go well. I was burned out, confused about my future, and quit. I took a little time off, and after sitting down with the course catalogue for a long time, I saw a program in gerontology, and I thought, *That's me—I love old people.*

"It took some time to figure out that helping could be my profession, but you keep asking yourself questions and that's how you figure things out."

Once Heather decided she wanted to be a nurse, she expected things would just fall into place, but they didn't. "I failed the major first-year nursing test by ten points," she recalled. "It was a major blow to my ego," she said. "I thought about quitting, but after a month I reminded myself that I'm not a quitter: I started again. You can't give up."

As she struggled to figure out her purpose, Heather said she learned about the core values that guide her: perseverance, helping others, and family.

After several years as a nurse—working everything from the postsurgical recovery room to labor and delivery—Heather is heading back to school for her master's degree. She's engaged to be married and thinking about the future. "School isn't my favorite thing, but since I hope to have a family, this degree will help me have the flexibility I need to both help others and be there for my family."

※ ※ ※

Your values guide your decisions, big and small. Values are what's important to you—what you cherish about yourself and your relationship with others. Values are about who you want to be, yet since your values are so much a part of your life, you might not see them until you really look.

Values drive the plot of the movie of your life, and research shows that identifying personal values is crucial for a life of purpose. "Questions pertaining to meaning and purpose for humans ultimately revolve around values, which can guide and define our lives," write JoAnne Dahl and her coauthors in *The Art and Science of Valuing in Psychotherapy*, a clinical guide for therapists. When you don't live a life that's consistent with your values, you may "feel like [your] life is lacking a sense of purpose or meaning, or that it is excessively painful."

Separating core values from the noise of life takes some reflection. Dr. Dahl writes that goals of achievement, status, income, possessions, and a particular type of physical beauty are not just held up as important by our society, but they are often marketed as values. They aren't. While you can certainly have goals without values, when you achieve those goals you're likely to feel pretty empty. Goals are best thought of as stepping-stones along our path to purpose, keeping us on track in our valued direction.

If one of your core values is friendship, a goal of organizing a weekend hiking trip with your best friends is a great stepping-stone to get there. Just organizing a hiking trip without your friends would seem a lot less meaningful for you.

This chapter is about exploring your values in a variety of different exercises. At first, the idea is just to brainstorm. Then you'll narrow it down and see how each of your values stack up against each other.

> *You know how if you plant seeds, it takes time for the fruits of the seeds to push up through the ground's surface? Same goes for the changes you want to manifest. Take the time to see. Seeing isn't believing. Seeding is believing. What you seed is what you get. If you seed positive thoughts and habits, success will eventually blossom for you.*
>
> —KAREN SALMANSOHN, AUTHOR

BRAINSTORMING ON YOUR VALUES

Dr. Dahl and her colleagues recommend identifying personal values in many dimensions of your life. I've adapted her dimensions here to fit with a young-adult life, but feel free to edit them further if you'd like. Don't just write single words. For each area, compose a sentence that describes the essence of your values. You can set up your statements as ways in which you want to act or be: "I want to keep myself open to the challenge of learning new things every day," or "I want to actively participate in my community by volunteering my time."

Remember to brainstorm on the big things that are important to you, rather than goals that relate to current stuff going on in your life.

Here is a sample to get you started:

Work	Value: I want to work at a job that both pays good money and makes a difference in my local community.
Family	Value: I want to give and receive love and support, in person as much as possible.
Romantic relationships	Value: I want to be in a relationship with open communication and mutual support.

EXERCISE 5.1

The Big Brainstorm

The left column below has a list of life categories. Use the right column to brainstorm about your values in those categories. If a category doesn't work for you, feel free to add your own, or skip ones that don't apply to your life right now.

Work

Value:

_____

_____

Free time

Value:

_____

_____

Family

Value:

_____

_____

Community involvement

Value:

_____

_____

Spirituality

Value:

_____

_____

Education   Value:

_____

_____

Body and health   Value:

_____

_____

Friends   Value:

_____

_____

Romantic relationships   Value:

_____

_____

Serving others   Value:

_____

_____

Look back at what you've written.

Here is another way to get to your values: choose from a researched list. Shalom Schwartz is a social psychologist who studies values. He created the following list of universal human values—values with which people worldwide identify.

EXERCISE 5.2

Universal Values List

Look at the list below and circle up to ten values that most resonate with you. Do some key words jump out at you? For the college students I know who tested these exercises, words like *independence, good health, love, helping people, honesty, friendship, support,* and *learning* were common ones to circle. In your personal list of values in many aspects of your life, what is most important to you? Circle those keywords. They are clues to deeper information about your value

Accepting one's position in life

Ambition

Authority

Beauty

Broad-mindedness

Capability

Choosing your own goals

Cleanliness

Creativity

Curiosity

Daring activities

Devoutness

Dominance

Enjoying life

Equality

Exciting life

Family security

Forgiveness

Freedom

Friendship

Health

Helpfulness

Honesty

Humility

Independence

Influence

Inner harmony

Intelligence

Leadership

Love

Loyalty

Moderation

National security

Obedience

Peace

Pleasure

Protecting the environment

Reciprocation of favors

Respect for tradition

Responsibility

Self-discipline

Self-respect

Sense of belonging

Social justice

Spirituality

Stability of social order

Success

Unity with nature

Varied life

Wisdom

Now, look back at what you circled in each of the two previous exercises and list the keywords and values in the space below. You'll come back to this list in a bit, so take some time to consolidate your ideas.

Keywords: Clues to My Core Values

_____	_____
_____	_____
_____	_____
_____	_____

* * *

Kimberly is a journalist and author. In her late twenties, she's passionate about communicating financial information to young adults in a way that's applicable to their lives. Initially inspired by Naomi Wolf's *Beauty Myth*, which she read at thirteen, Kimberly worked her way up in journalism and has published several books.

Climbing the ladder in any career comes with its fair share of rejection, but for writers, the more successful you are, the more you get rejected—because you are always submitting material, constantly putting yourself out there, and pushing for the next big idea. For Kimberly, learning to deal with the rejection and feelings of failure after a string of "Thanks, but I'll pass" emails from editors has been one of the biggest challenges early in her career.

Letting go of the "shoulds" was the other big challenge: In her early twenties, a mentor told Kimberly to do what she wanted to do, not what she felt she was "supposed to do" when it came to picking a career. "Perseverance is easier when you are working toward a passion, not just another item on the to-do list," she said.

At the start of her career, Kimberly felt like she had to focus on being famous. "Now it's about having a positive impact on other people's lives, including my own family." Her advice to others: "Forget about all of the stuff that you feel like you 'should' do . . . and just focus on the activities that truly feel meaningful to you and that you can lose yourself in. Those are the ones you will continue to love and improve in, and where you'll be willing to face the inevitable failures and setbacks."

✳ ✳ ✳

As you ponder your values, you undoubtedly will enter the realm of the shoulds. *Shoulds* come from the peanut gallery of friends, family, society, and your own cultural background. They are the statements you hear about what's good and bad, right and wrong:

▸ You *should* go to a four-year college.
▸ You *should* major in something that will give you a direct career path to success.
▸ You *should* take the job that pays the most.

Shoulds also come in the "have to" and "must" varieties:

▸ You *have to* have a date for your cousin's wedding.
▸ You *must* dress in a certain way to worship.
▸ You *have to* get a roommate because living alone isn't safe.

> *We have all been placed on this Earth to discover our own path, and*
> *we will never be happy if we live someone else's idea of life.*
> —JAMES VAN PRAAGH, AUTHOR AND TELEVISION PERSONALITY

You may already be in a purpose mindset, suggests Barbara Braham in her book *Finding Your Purpose*. You may know what your values are or how you want to live them, yet you still might not be doing them because you are caught up in what she calls the "tyranny of the shoulds."

It's the people we care about most—people whom we love, respect, and admire—who will give us the most confining should-based advice. And we want to listen, because not only do we want to please them, we worry that they are right, and we must be wrong.

We can still ask for people's advice and opinions; at many points in your journey of purpose, you'll do just that. But beware of statements that begin with "You should . . ." or "You have to . . ." or "You must . . ."—even from me and these worksheets—because that advice might not be in line with your values.

The most insidious of the shoulds are your own. Because of the way we are socialized, we all have ideas about the right way to act, dress, work, express our feelings, and have fun. Yet different cultures socialize people differently. Correct behavior in China might seem weird in Canada. The proper way to dress in one neighborhood might be totally inappropriate in another.

Your shoulds are different from my shoulds, which means that they are up for debate, discussion, and perhaps even disposal.

Braham puts shoulds into three categories:

▶ Having shoulds are the things that we think we need for a good life—a certain kind of car, a job that pays a specific amount of money, or this season's fashionable clothes.

▶ Doing shoulds are the ways we think we need to act, like watching less TV and reading more, spending more time at the gym, or having a more active social life.

▶ Being shoulds are our ideas about how we want people to think about us—that we are smart, organized, funny, or perfect.

"Forget what you are supposed to do. Do what you want to do."
—SOMETHING BORROWED (2011)

EXERCISE 5.3

Shoulds vs. Values

Think of the shoulds/musts/have-tos in the big areas of your life (listed below). Take a moment to jot them down. Be honest here. What do you feel pressured to do, be, or have in each area?

| Family | Education | Work | Physical |
| Financial | Spiritual | Relationships | Free time |

Family

_____

_____

Education

_____

_____

Work

_____

_____

Physical

_____

_____

Financial

_____

_____

Spiritual

_____

_____

Relationships

_____

_____

Free time

_____

_____

You'll probably never let go of all your shoulds, but by acknowledging the shoulds that you feel, you can begin to separate them from your core values.

Remember that not all shoulds, have-tos, and musts are bad. (You should call your elderly relatives more often. You have to shower occasionally. You must eat.) But reframing a should as a value allows us to take more personal control, and that's what we do next.

Look back at your list of shoulds, and see which ones might be rephrased into values that are important to you. Here's Lyndsay's list, where she reframes her common shoulds into personal values:

Should	Value
I should work out more.	I value staying in shape, so I should do some type of physical activity every day. This doesn't necessarily have to be going to the gym.
I should read more.	I value intelligence, so I should read the newspaper to stay informed and novels to improve my vocabulary.
I should save more money.	I value wealth, so I should save the money I receive on my paychecks and spend the money I receive in tips.
I should keep a clean house.	I value cleanliness, so I should pick up after myself constantly so that it never gets to the point of being messy.

EXERCISE 5.4

Reframing Shoulds as Values

Take your biggest shoulds and reframe them as values, as Lyndsay did above.

Should   Value

_____   _____

_____   _____

_____   _____

If you need some help translating your shoulds into values, here's a list of what some student-testers came up with to get their values in order.

I Should . . .	Really, What I Value Is . . .
Be caring	Love/compassion
Be fit	Health
Be friends with my siblings	Family/support
Be harder working	Success
Be less bossy	Equality/balance
Be kinder	Kindness
Be more romantic	Relationships/love
Be present at family events	Family/support
Be punctual	Respect
Do more housework	Cleanliness
Eat three meals a day	Health
Enjoy exciting activities	Activity/adventure/friendship
Exercise	Health
Find a job	Financial stability
Get something out of every class	Awareness/knowledge
Go to church	Presentation/reputation/faith
Have a healthy body	Health
Have a wider friend network	Friendship
Have an enjoyable job	Competency
Have fun	Passions/things I love
Invest in the stock market	Accountability/experience
Maintain good relationships	Loyalty/honesty
Relax	Relaxation
Save money	Restraint/responsibility
Sleep more	Health
Spend less time on the Internet	Important things in life
Spend time with family	Family
Spending "me" time	Independence
Stay focused	Achievement
Study more	Education

▣ YOUR VALUES BRACKET

After the shoulds exercise, go back and look at your list of values on page 71. Are any of those values actually shoulds, have-tos, or musts? With each value, ask yourself, *Do I really, honestly care about this, or is this just a way for me to pat myself on the back for being "good"? Are these values for me to live my real life by—or are they for some idealized person who doesn't exist?*

One way to figure out which values are most important is to, quite literally, play them off of each other.

Do you fill out a college basketball bracket during March Madness? Welcome to Values Madness—your chance to figure out what core values drive you, from the Sweet Sixteen to the Final Four.

First, you'll identify your values in four "conferences"—personal, social, achievement, and physical values. Then you'll pit them against each other in a simple bracket-based competition.

This exercise might sound a bit daft—like you are comparing apples and oranges—but life often asks us to choose among our values. You can create as many brackets as you want and play around with this idea until you are comfortable. What's more, you can stop at the Final Four or take it all the way until you reach your one core, champion value. It's up to you.

Step 1: Establish the Conferences

In his book *Now What? The Young Person's Guide to Choosing the Perfect Career*, Nicholas Lore presents readers with four lists of values, which we use below, to prompt their thinking: personal, social, achievement and physical values. Look back at your list from page 71 and start by transferring those core values into each category below. Add more as you think of them. The goal will be to narrow them down to four in each conference, but you can start with a longer list if necessary.

Personal values guide your personal conduct. For example, you might include friendship, seeking the truth, independence, compassion, and excellence. On the other hand, you might describe your primary personal values as self-discipline, tradition, loyalty, empathy, and leadership.

My personal values are:

_____   _____

_____   _____

_____   _____

_____   _____

Social values guide the choice of people you spend time with, and the culture and environment in which you thrive. You might include belonging to the group, conservative/traditional, family, patriotism, and competition. Another person might choose values of tolerance of differences, obeying an inner authority, passion, progressive morals, and freedom.

My social values are:

_____   _____

_____   _____

_____   _____

_____   _____

Achievement values spur you into action. What motivates you to achieve your goals? These values might include the idea that big changes start small, it's good to do more with less, leaving a legacy, or living life to the fullest. Maybe you're driven by entrepreneurship, philanthropy, fame, making the world a better place, being daring, and the desire to invent.

My achievement values are:

_____   _____

_____   _____

_____   _____

_____   _____

Physical values guide your decisions relating to physical things—be it your body, money, or technological toys. Are you guided by beauty, elegance, the latest fashions, quality, and urban living? Or perhaps it's a desire for interesting experiences, holistic living, and casual, comfortable, and organic styles. Whether you save or spend, whether you want the latest gadgets or value fixing broken things, values about things can be a driving force in your life, too.

My physical values are:

_____   _____

_____   _____

_____   _____

_____   _____

Step 2: Narrow It Down

Now go back through and circle the top four values in each of the four categories or conferences.

Write your values down in groups of four—first list your personal values, then your social values, then your achievement values, and finally your physical values—to create your Sweet Sixteen list.

Step 3: Start Playing the Values against Each Other

Compare each conference's values with the other values in that conference. Which is more important to you? In the match-up between friendship and independence, for example, which value wins? There will be some close decisions, but even if the match goes into overtime, a victor must be declared.

Do this for each of the conferences.

By the time you get to the Final Four, you'll be pitting your top value in each of the conferences against each other. You could stop there if you wanted to, but try to push yourself to see what wins out in the end.

> Danny researches companies and produces reports intended to guide investors in their purchasing and selling decisions. But not all the companies he researches do business in a way that matches his personal value system. "Honesty, integrity, and accountability come into play," Danny said. Frequently in the high-pressure financial world, these values are challenged—whether it's because of the actions of a company he is covering or a subtle request to advise investors toward something he doesn't believe is correct. "It may seem as if going against these morals will result in 'success.' However, I believe those options are always short term in nature. Long term, they are wrong decisions." Danny knows his achievement values—both in a personal and professional sense. What are yours?

Figure 5.1. Your Values Bracket

Of the values that made it to the Final Four, which are your top three values? That's a tough one, but try your best. Write these down in your movie reel in Appendix B.

◼ ALIGNING ACTIONS AND VALUES

Now that you've got a list of your core values—and a sense for how they might play out when they are pitted against each other in competition—how can you make sure your actions are in line with those core values?

In his book *Mere Christianity*, C. S. Lewis writes that we waste too much time worrying about *how* we are going to make ourselves have charitable feelings toward others. Instead, he says, just do it.

> The rule for all of us is perfectly simple. Do not waste time bothering whether you "love" your neighbor; act as if you did. As soon as we do this, we find one of the great secrets. When you are behaving as if you loved someone, you will presently come to love him. If you injure someone you dislike, you will find yourself disliking him more.

The same goes for living your values. If you align your actions to make sure you are living your values, you will feel more purposeful. If you ignore your values, follow the crowd or the shoulds, or doubt your true beliefs, you will feel less purposeful. To maximize values-based, purposeful living, keep what matters front and center in your mind:

- ▶ Write your values on the back of a business card or on the back of an index card cut to the size of a credit card and stick it near the money or credit cards in your wallet. Then, every time you open your wallet, you'll see your values.
- ▶ Tape your values to the mirror above your dresser or on your computer, or make it the lock-screen on your phone.
- ▶ Make your most central value the password to your computer or email—a password that you use at least once a day.
- ▶ Enter your values as reminders in your personal calendars.

*Nothing is given to man on earth—struggle is built into the nature of life,
and conflict is possible—the hero is the man who lets no obstacle prevent
him for pursuing the values he has chosen.*

—ANDREW BERNSTEIN, PHILOSOPHER

❊ ❊ ❊

You've done some great work here identifying your strengths, talents, skills, values and passions. Take a moment now, if you haven't already, to list the most important ones in your movie reel.

If you skimmed this section, consider going back and doing the exercises now. The rest of the book builds on these strengths and values. You'll refer back to them a few more times. And up next, we get to the "big" stuff: Your vision and your purpose—and your commitments for making it happen.

Take a deep breath and let's continue on our journey:
Onward toward purpose!

Part 2

Vision, Purpose, and . . . Action!

CHAPTER 6

Passions in Action

As a child, Kristie wanted to be a dancer. She took her first ballet classes at age four, and by age twelve she was enrolled in a performing arts school and fell in love with modern dance. But during her freshman year of college, she began passing out while dancing. Doctors identified a rare congenital heart disorder, and Kristie was immediately medicated.

Wearing a monitor around her chest to detect and record quickened heartbeats, Kristie kept dancing. A year or so after her initial diagnosis, the monitor began to beep. Her boyfriend caught her as she fell to the ground. The doctor was concerned but said Kristie could wait until Monday to come in for an exam, and she danced all weekend. After an initial exam, her doctor sent her into emergency surgery for a pacemaker. He was shocked to see that her heart rate had been clocked at four hundred beats per minute—typically a fatal situation if left to continue.

A pacemaker would save her life, but a pacemaker would also mean she couldn't dance.

In college, Kristie had double-majored in modern dance and elementary education, her plan B in case she had to get a pacemaker. As she prepared for surgery, she cried. "Well, Dad, I guess it's plan B," she said. "And that was the last time I cried about it."

"I put it all into a little box," Kristie said. "I realize now that I went into a deep depression. My boyfriend at the time—who is now my husband—was a stage manager, and I couldn't go to his shows. I would cry for days. I tried to do more low-impact dance classes, but it made me angry not to be able to move like I used to. I basically stopped moving at that point."

Soon after, she married, became pregnant, and then miscarried. "I lost a lot of faith in my body," she said. When she became pregnant again, she knew that she needed to move again—in some way that was appropriate for her—to ensure the baby's health. She began yoga. Once her son was born, she began to breastfeed and to have some more faith in her body's abilities.

In addition to being a full-time mom, Kristie was going nonstop as she cleaned houses, baked cakes, and started nannying for another child in her home. "My son was my first passion since dancing. I wasn't taking my medicines, doing yoga, or taking care of myself."

One day, as she was loading her son and the little girl she cared for into the car, her pacemaker shocked her five times, dropping her to her knees in the pouring rain. "It was a clear sign I needed to take my medicines and take care of myself again, but other things happened, too. I had panic attacks whenever I went to drive. I associated the car and driving with the trauma. I needed help, and I started therapy."

At twenty-seven, Kristie began psychological counseling to fully face the loss of her identity as a dancer. "I had to figure out what I wanted to do when I grew up. I was pregnant with my second child and had no idea what was going to come next. I thought about my love of baking cakes, and I was gifted at making costumes for kids. I bounced from one idea to the next for a while, until I began yoga again."

Kristie investigated what she needed to do to become a yoga instructor. "I couldn't afford the training, but I was able to work off the class time. Every obstacle in my way was getting cleared. After my daughter was born, I wanted to nurse her, and I was able to build a work and teaching schedule that allowed for that, too.

"I was learning again. I loved to learn what happens when your body moves. And I was empowered. I wasn't 'Mom' in this setting. I was Kristie. All my knowledge of anatomy from years of dancing and studying movement in dance came back to me. It was like picking up an old hat: It fit perfectly."

✳ ✳ ✳

So far in this book, you've already invested a lot of time listing your talents, strengths, and skills. You separated your shoulds from your values and came up with a short list that you want to guide your life. Are you feeling pretty good about yourself? I hope so. Whether your belief system tells you that these are gifts from God, the universe, Mother Nature, or just plain good luck, your task now is twofold: to be grateful, and to give back.

Just as Kristie discovered that her childhood passions could lead to a purposeful life, even on a path different from one she'd originally envisioned, this chapter is intended to help you think about your passions and how you can use your gifts to make a difference to others on a micro and a macro level. As you craft the movie of your life, we are now getting to the nitty-gritty of the plot itself—the characteristics that will drive your life forward with purpose.

What do you love to do? This question isn't about what you actually do in a day. It's to prompt you to think about what makes you happy, what gives you meaning, and what makes you feel fulfilled. We all have different interests and passions, and only by recognizing them can we get on the path of giving our gifts to others.

So take a journey back in time, before the tyranny of the shoulds took over your life. What does your inner kid have to tell you about doing what you love? Think back to a happy age—maybe it's age ten or twelve, or even a bit younger. Did you love watching the Discovery Channel? Were you happiest when you were eating ice cream? As you ask yourself these questions, it's okay to smile or laugh as you write. In fact, I'd encourage it.

A man's maturity: that is to have rediscovered the seriousness he possessed as a child at play.
—FRIEDRICH NIETZSCHE, PHILOSOPHER

EXERCISE 6.1

What Does Your Inner Kid Tell You about Doing What You Love?

What made you happy at age ten?

_____

_____

_____

What did you like to do for fun? What were your favorite toys?

_____

_____

_____

What did you want to be when you grew up?

_____

_____

_____

What fascinated you?

_____

_____

_____

"All my life needed was a sense of someplace to go." —TAXI (2004)

Now bring yourself back to the present day. What are the adult versions of the stuff you loved to do as a kid? Are you interested in those now? For example, let's say you wanted to be a firefighter. If that's still a passion for you, your local volunteer fire company might be a good place to check out—and even if not as a firefighter, perhaps as an occasional volunteer at the station. But press that idea further: What was it that you thought was cool about being a firefighter when you were a kid? Rescuing others? The fire itself? The adrenaline rush of the work?

Jordyne writes that when she was younger, she wanted to be a mother, and she still loves to work with children. "Many of my jobs have been at camps and daycares. I am currently volunteering with disabled children. My current career goal is occupational therapy, and as of now, my dream would be to work in this field with kids."

Take a moment to think about how your childhood loves might provide clues to your adult purpose. Jot some notes here.

Inner Kid Snapshot: Lyndsay

What made you happy at age ten?

I used to get so excited after rainstorms to go outside and jump in puddles. Playing with animals made me extremely happy. I loved getting stickers to add to my sticker book/collection. Ice cream, candy, and cookies could always cheer me up!

What did you like to do for fun?

At age ten I enjoyed playing house with my friends and pretending I was the mother of the family. We also frequently played school, and I liked being the teacher. I also liked to play with Barbies and drive around in my Barbie jeep. I liked to play dress-up with my mom's old clothes and my dance costumes.

What did you want to be when you grew up?

At the age of ten my career choice changed almost every other week. Some professions I considered were being an astronaut, a veterinarian, a professional dancer, and a teacher. For a brief period of time I was certain I would grow up to be Ariel from *The Little Mermaid*.

What fascinated you?

I was fascinated by onstage productions and performances. I used to be in awe of New York City and the ocean. Hide-and-go-seek was one of the most fascinating games I had ever played. Macaroni art and coloring mesmerized me for hours. My parents used to drive me around to look at all the neighborhood house lights and decorations around Christmastime.

How do your childhood loves provide clues to your adult purpose?

I think my idea of being a teacher stemmed from the facts that I like to have control over situations and organize my thoughts and materials my own way. I still do believe that being an astronaut would be a cool profession, however. I think it's more the mystery and risk aspects that made it so appealing. My fascination with New York City sort of supports my choice to move from a suburban area to attend school in Pittsburgh. Also, I think my love for the Christmas lights extended beyond aesthetics. I think I liked the idea of unity within our neighborhood to celebrate one single event.

If you're looking for more guidance about what you love to do, the list in Exercise 6.2, which is adapted from Carol Adrienne's *The Purpose of Your Life*, is certainly not comprehensive, but it should start you on creating your own list of passions.

EXERCISE 6.2

Your Passions

1. Go through the list and circle activities that appeal to you.
2. Challenge yourself to add a few of your own.
3. Finally, create two lists: one list of activities you want to do every day and a second list of activities you want to do at least occasionally.

Advise	Discuss	Have fun	Persuade	Spend time with family
Advocate	Drive	Heal	Pray	Stare out the window
Analyze	Eat	Inspire	Problem solve	
Bake	Edit	Interact with people	Produce	Stretch
Beautify	Email		Read	Surf
Bike	Encourage	Laugh	Record	Talk
Campaign	Entertain	Learn	Renovate	Teach
Care for others	Exercise	Listen	Repair	Text message
Collect	Explore	Listen to music	Reveal	Tinker
Cook	Facebook chat	Meditate	Run	Travel
Create	Fashion	Mentor	Sail	Volunteer
Critique	Feed	Negotiate	Sing	Walk
Dance	Garden	Nurture	Sleep	Win
Daydream	Go out with friends	Organize	Solve problems	Write
Direct		Paint		
Discover	Guide	People watch		

Your additions to the list

_____   _____   _____   _____   _____

_____   _____   _____   _____   _____

_____   _____   _____   _____   _____

Things I Want to Do Every Day

1. _____

2. _____

3. _____

4. _____

5. _____

Things I Want to Do Occasionally

1. _____

2. _____

3. _____

4. _____

5. _____

Of these, what are the three top things you love to do? Write these down in your movie reel in Appendix B.

◼ MAKING A POSITIVE CONTRIBUTION

Now look over these lists—what you loved to do as a child, how those activities may have informed what you can do as an adult based on those interests, and the activities that now fill you with passion. With this perspective on your own life, what might you be able to do that would make your community or the world a better place?

For example, if you love to talk, you might advocate for causes. If you love to explore and discover unknown things, a career in the physical sciences might be a good fit. And if you love talking and listening to people, a counseling profession might work well.

Being as specific as possible, create one more list with your values and passions in mind.

EXERCISE 6.3

Things I Love to Do That Might Contribute to Society

_____

_____

_____

Prioritizing Your Passions

Real life is about figuring out the right mix of passions, career, and family time—balancing responsibilities, fun, and personal care. Try Exercise 6.4, created by *Big Picture* tester Joey Mazarella, to see how you can prioritize your passions while still living a full, productive life.

EXERCISE 6.4

Passion Management

Step 1. List below your favorite hobbies, passions, interests (look back at the previous pages), and career aspirations. (Joey's completed exercise is interspersed here as an example.)

Passions and Interests   *Career Aspirations*

_____   _____

_____   _____

_____   _____

_____   _____

_____   _____

For example, Joey's chart looked like this:

Passions and Interests   *Career Aspirations*

Fitness _____   Army Nursing _____

Research _____

Helping others _____

Family _____

Friends _____

Sleep ☺ _____

Step 2. Now fill in how many waking hours a week you hope to dedicate to these passions, interests, and career aspirations. Keep in mind that it's okay to have more time spent on hobbies than a job, if that's what floats your boat right now. Also keep in mind that you need sleep. If you get eight hours a night of sleep, you're down to 112 hours in the week. Divide those 112 hours up (and include more sleep or downtime in there, too, if you want to take some naps).

As an example, Joey's chart looked like this:

Passions, Interests, Career Aspirations	Percentage of My 112 Hours of Time
Fitness	15
Research	10
Helping others	5
Army Nursing	40
Family	20
Sleep	5
Friends	5

Now fill in your own: (see next page)

Passions, Interests, Career Aspirations	*Percentage of My 112 Hours of Time*
_____	_____
_____	_____
_____	_____
_____	_____
_____	_____
_____	_____

Step 3. Spend a few minutes reflecting on these charts.

Is this going to be exactly how you spend your time? No. But it's a good guide to help you figure out what's important to you. If you're noticing, for example, that you want to dedicate a significant chunk of time to a non career-related passion, it's important to consider how that will practically work in the life you are building for yourself.

As necessary, reevaluate how you wish to dedicate your time to your different passions. Try to find connections between your hobbies and career paths that may link them together. There are no right or wrong answers—and again, you're not locking yourself into a specific plan. But this exercise can be very instructive as you begin to think about the proper balance between your career and other passions.

After doing this exercise himself, Joey wrote that he had a better idea about how he wanted to spend his time. "After sleep and family, I wish to dedicate a lot of my free time to fitness and research. Judging by this, it may be a better idea to choose a career path in nursing that will allow me to have extra free time to spend on my personal fitness, research, and helping others through personal training or volunteering."

Jot down any thoughts or reactions here:

_____

_____

_____

_____

Focusing too much on unrealistic passions won't set you up for a realistic adult life. At the same time, ignoring those cues entirely isn't a recipe for thriving either. You've taken a smart approach to putting passions into action so far by not just thinking about what you love to do, but how those passions might be used to benefit society—and now you're headed a bit deeper by exploring your vision for change. Hold on to those passions and dreams as the plot thickens ahead.

CHAPTER 7

A Vision for Change

A person starts to live when he can live outside himself.
—ALBERT EINSTEIN

Life's most urgent question is, What are you doing for others?
—MARTIN LUTHER KING JR.

SERVICE IS THE GIFT OF SHARING OURSELVES—our gifts, our love, our knowledge—with others. Service isn't just helping the needy—it's doing our jobs, whatever they are, as well as possible, and living our lives with others in mind.

You can serve others every day, especially while doing things that are interesting to you or activities you love. If you work in manufacturing, service means making sure the screws are on tight. If you volunteer at a home for at-risk kids, it means playing board games and showing it's okay to be silly. If you work in an office, it means making sure that the data is entered correctly. If you've got a sibling, it means supporting them and sharing a fun activity. If you are driving, it means letting someone pull in front of you.

For example, Xin says she serves others through small daily actions like riding her bicycle instead of driving, bringing environmental bags with her when she grocery shops, and being honest when people ask her a question. Just smiling makes a big difference, too.

An ocean of bliss may rain down from the heavens,
but if you only hold up a thimble, that is all you receive.
—RAMAKRISHNA, INDIAN MYSTIC

And generosity to those less fortunate can also make you smile. Laura says she sometimes buys dinner for a man who sits outside her local pharmacy. "It costs me five dollars, and I know this makes his night better. It gives him food and the knowledge that someone has noticed and cared about him. Plus, after I buy him dinner, he always tells me I'm beautiful and says, 'God bless you.'"

And who knows where the ripple effects of a good deed end? Indeed, the little ways you use your talents, strengths, and skills to help others can make a big difference. Some people call this the "butterfly effect" or "chaos theory." This familiar proverb dates back to the fourteenth century:

> For want of a nail the shoe was lost.
> For want of a shoe the horse was lost.
> For want of a horse the rider was lost.
> For want of a rider the message was lost.
> For want of a message the battle was lost.
> For want of a battle the kingdom was lost.
> And all for the want of a horseshoe nail.

What little thing might you do that could have big consequences? Hold the elevator door for someone perhaps? The proverb could go like this:

> For want of an elevator, the train was lost.
> For want of a train, the class was lost.
> For want of a class, the exam was lost.
> For want of an exam, the A-grade was lost.
> For want of an A, the job offer was lost.
> And all for the want of an elevator.

There's evidence that we feel richer when we give back to others, just another side effect in that butterfly theory. As I mentioned earlier in the book, psychologists have found that prosocial spending—spending on friends or giving to charity—makes us happier for longer than buying things for ourselves. According to a Harvard study, people who give to charity are 43 percent more likely than people who don't give to say they're very happy people. But this idea of giving doesn't necessarily mean money: People who give blood are twice as likely to say they're very happy people as people who don't. People who volunteer are happier. Study after study seems to show that contribution of any kind boosts happiness because it decreases stress.

How are you called to contribute and change the world? That's where your vision comes in—the driving theme of the movie of your life. And now it's time to think big.

Crystallize Your Vision

A vision is your hope for the future, your dream of what could be possible. It's your call to service, to help others, and to effect social change that makes the world a better place. Your vision is a problem that needs to be solved, a yearning that needs to be filled—and one that calls out to you more than others. Your vision is outward focused, and while it's bigger than you, it's possible to accomplish (or partially accomplish) with passion and planning.

Unfortunately, this big vision doesn't usually come personally addressed to you via email or text message. It also doesn't come with instructions. In those early moments, a vision is an amorphous feeling that something needs to change—and that you might be the one to make it happen.

I say "might be" because one of the pesky things about visions is that they seem to go hand in hand with self-doubt over whether it would be possible to achieve such a lofty goal of contribution to society. Later we'll talk about ways to push past these moments of self-doubt, but for now, just know that as you brainstorm about your possible vision, there might be a nagging voice that says "that's pointless," or "that will never work," or "you're not smart or skilled enough to do that." Ignore those for now. Just brainstorm. Think big. Dream big. We'll get to the nitty-gritty later.

> *The only ones among you who will be happy are those*
> *who will have sought and found how to serve.*
> —ALBERT SCHWEITZER, THEOLOGIAN, MUSICIAN, PHYSICIAN

EXERCISE 7.1

An Inspirational Visionary

To get you dreaming big, start by thinking of a visionary person—living or dead, someone you know or someone you've read about—who has lived a life of purpose and meaning.

It doesn't have to be anyone famous. One student wrote that her friend takes a bus thirty minutes each way to volunteer at a nursing home so that she can serve tea and play bingo with the residents. This type of service is inspiring.

Who is your visionary person?

_____

What did that person do to serve others and leave and make the world a better place?

_____

_____

How, specifically, did that person do it?

_____

_____

Perhaps this person's vision is one that you share. But the goal here isn't to take on a vision that seems worthy. Plenty of problems in the world are calling out for a solution, and you're not going to be able to fix them all. Now that you're in the vision mindset, the goal is to find *your* vision and to figure out what speaks to you more than anything else right now.

A variety of catalysts can inspire your vision. In their book *Live Your Calling*, Kevin and Kay Marie Brennfleck divide these into three big categories: need-driven, design-driven, and experience-driven visions.

Need-driven visions are created by your desire to solve a need or problem. Perhaps you are called to help victims of an earthquake get the long-term care they need to rebuild their lives. Perhaps you see the frustration of your grandparents as they try to communicate and keep in touch with family members, so you use your knowledge of technology to help them—and the elderly in your community as a whole—join the digital age.

Design-driven visions emerge when you seek to use your particular gifts to live your purpose. Let's say you've got skills in working with physical things, you're good with details, and you are gifted at managing and persuading people. You could use those gifts to pursue a career as a teacher or trainer of hands-on skills, the head of a start-up company providing affordable housing, or perhaps as a mentor or coach for kids.

Experience-driven visions rise from your own life story and the challenges you or others close to you have overcome. During her treatment for breast cancer, Elissa, who we meet later in this book, decided that she wanted to retain her femininity during the radiation process by wearing a different dress to each session. She posted photos online and on Facebook of herself and her "thirty-three dresses project" journey. Thousands of women began to follow her story, citing her posts as the inspiration they needed to stay positive during their own cancer treatments. The American Cancer Society recognized Elissa for her efforts, and, now cancer-free, she's speaking to other survivors about the power of positive attitudes in a time of struggle.

Your vision ideas may fall into one or all of these categories. But the important thing is that the vision is yours—and that it speaks to you, your passions, and your hopes for the future. To begin brainstorming, spend some time jotting down notes on these questions below.

> *Owning our story can be hard but not nearly as difficult as spending our lives running from it. Embracing our vulnerabilities is risky but not nearly as dangerous as giving up on love and belonging and joy—the experiences that make us the most vulnerable. Only when we are brave enough to explore the darkness will we discover the infinite power of our light.*
> —BRENÉ BROWN, AUTHOR, PUBLIC SPEAKER

■ VISION QUESTS

Seekers have embarked on vision quests for millennia. A traditional vision quest is a Native American rite of passage—something undertaken during the transition to adulthood—and was a time of fasting and insight. For modern young-adults, let's think of vision quests as a time of exploration.

That's what this exercise is all about: exploring during your transition into adulthood. Take some time to reflect on what captures your attention and to explore a variety of different needs in society. Whether your vision is need driven, design-driven, or experience-driven, these vision quests will expand your thinking.

EXERCISE 7.2

Vision Quest A: What's the News?

So many news stories present bad news. Your vision may be to right wrongs and step in to help those in need. Perhaps you are drawn to stories of mistreatment or hate crimes because you want to learn more about how you can help prevent them. Maybe you're drawn to stories of people overcoming obstacles because you find them inspiring.

What kinds of news stories get your attention? Start with the general and then get specific: If it's stories about politics, does local or national politics interest you more? Are there particular issues that hold your attention? Why? Whom do they impact?

EXERCISE 7.3

Vision Quest B: What's the Trend

Picture yourself standing in front of a magazine rack or scrolling through websites: What magazine do you grab? What site do you gravitate toward? Why? What interests you about the contents of that print or online magazine? What specific articles or stories or pictures spark your interest?

If your initial reaction is, "Well, I mostly read magazines at the gym or on an airplane, and I grab *Cosmopolitan* or *Sports Illustrated* or *US Weekly*, so that's not very helpful," think again. Don't dismiss your interest in popular magazines. Meaning-making meaning doesn't have to be dire and depressing.

=Really think about what media you like to look at—and why. Are you interested in the current fashion trends? Could this spark an idea about vision for you? Are you interested in athlete profiles? What might this tell you about your passion for people and their inspirational success?

EXERCISE 7.4

Vision Quest C: What's the Challenge

Chris is a pediatric nurse who specializes in palliative care for infants and children and care for families with special needs. While she knew from a young age that she wanted to be a nurse, Chris believes God revealed his purpose for her when her daughter, Lindsay, was born with a chromosomal disorder and died before her third birthday, and her second daughter, Kara, was born prematurely. After spending time with both children in the neonatal intensive-care unit, and experiencing the devastating loss of a child, Chris knew that she could take the pain—and the lessons she learned—and help others in similar situations.

Describing her experience-based vision of supportive care for children and families in need, Chris said that "not everyone is cut out for palliative care, but I've been there, so I understand. I'm there for parents because I know what they are going though. I can't make the decisions for them, but I can support them." To be a great nurse, she said, "You have to care about other people. You have to have empathy and you have to experience it—it can't be taught."

Have you or a family member learned to live with or overcome an illness, addiction, disability, or other challenge? Are you passionate about educating others in that arena? Describe briefly your experiences:

_____

_____

_____

EXERCISE 7.5

Vision Quest D: What's the Need?

Sam was a residential advisor during his sophomore year at a large state university. He loved the job, loved his staff, and loved working with the students. In the spring semester, a student named Travis transferred from a nearby state school. He was artistic, kind, sporty, and shy. Sam remembers connecting to him—reading beside him, but speaking little—and feeling his loneliness.

"The year was wrapping up," Sam wrote. "I was on target for straight As. But then I was thrust into the world of suicide. The introduction was unforeseen and abrupt. Travis died by suicide in the parking lot of the residence hall. I remember being there as the officers said he was dead. I remember seeing his lifeless body. And I most certainly remember the hole that occupied the place where his heart once beat vigorously.

"I was haunted by the explicit images of death. Acute stress disorder became posttraumatic stress disorder as the months passed. I saw him in similar-faced people. I imagined his car in the parking lot as I walked out of my building. Nightmares, crying fits, and my own thoughts of death took over. By the following winter, I was a mess. I pushed away my then-girlfriend and imagined driving my parents' car off a cliff. Before I ended my own life I checked into the nearest hospital and was immediately placed under a seventy-two-hour hold."

Sam had hit bottom. After he was released from the hospital, he sought shelter with family and friends, and while those months were challenging, he said he was filled with a new energy—and a life purpose. "I saw an inherent need to change what I experienced—or at least make a difference."

Sam founded and raised more than $27,000 for the Always Remember Never Surrender Scholarship Endowment that works to combat suicide. He organized campus-awareness events for suicide prevention, began to pursue research in suicide prevention, and eventually joined the Alliance for Suicide Prevention in his county.

Recently, at an Alliance for Suicide Prevention fundraising walk, Sam met a man who was struggling with the loss to suicide of a person close to him. "The man sat next to me. I said nothing. He was crying without end. After a few minutes, I placed my hand on his back and said, 'You're safe here.' He continued to cry, but I remained persistent in my attempts to help. At first it was single words . . . 'I'm . . . depressed.' I kept asking questions. Red flags screamed in my head.

And then he said it, 'I want to kill myself. Now! I can't do this anymore.' Immediately I kicked into gear, called the police, and a mental-health check was given. He was taken by ambulance to a nearby facility. I don't know the rest of his story. What I do know is that I'm passionate about saving lives. My goal is to be able to do what I could not with Travis. In that moment of crisis and need, I want to be able to say, 'There's another way. There's help in this moment of darkness.'"

Sam has found the folks who need his help the most. Who needs your help? Name at least one person in your family, neighborhood, nation, and the world who has it harder than you do right now, and write down why and how—and then how you might be able to make it a bit better for that person.

Family Member _____

Maybe it's your mother, father, or grandparent. For example, Alexa is amazed by her mother, who is working multiple jobs to pay for Alexa's education—and Alexa knows she can help by working hard so she can provide for her mom after graduation. Maybe it's your elderly grandfather whose mind is starting to go. Who in your family has it harder than you do? What could you do to make that life better?

_____

_____

_____

Neighborhood _____

Perhaps your neighbor's spouse died recently. Perhaps a friend in your neighborhood is being teased for being different. Could you visit the lonely widow or help combat bullying in your area? Think about those in your community and ask yourself: *Why and how do they have it harder than I do?* What could you do to make that life better?

_____

_____

_____

Nation _____

Are you concerned about the homeless? Perhaps you might consider volun-teering at a soup kitchen. Do you recognize the challenges in your local public school system? Might you donate time or books to help out? Nationally, who has it harder than you? What could you do to make that life better?

_____

_____

_____

World _____

Are you captivated by a particular country or people plagued by war? Perhaps you're interested in those who are struggling with poverty or famine. There are so many causes in the world, but which speak to you the most? Often it's hardest to do something about them on a grand scale, but small efforts can mean big changes in individual lives. Thinking about those people affected, why and how do they have it harder than you do? What could you do to make that life better?

_____

_____

_____

A person without a purpose is like a ship without a rudder.
—THOMAS CARLYLE, PHILOSOPHER AND TEACHER

■ DO WHAT YOU LOVE

Look back through the notes you've taken so far—especially in Exercise 6.3 on page 95—and your answers in the vision quests. What themes are emerging? What ideas recur? Are there ways you can do what you love while living out a vision for change among your family, community, and beyond?

If you love to hike, perhaps you can live out a vision of exploring nature and teaching others about its beauty. Let's say you love cooking. Well, you are feeding people—and that's a vision in itself.

EXERCISE 7.6

Live Your Vision of Change

By doing _____ ,

I can live out my vision of _____

_____ .

By doing _____ ,

I can live out my vision of _____

_____ .

By doing _____ ,

I can live out my vision of _____

_____ .

Of all the ideas you've brainstormed about in this chapter—all the problems that concern you, all the ways you might help others, all the things you love to do—which one speaks to you most? Let that one guide your vision statement.

Sara writes that she wants to see a world in which retirement, nursing homes, and aging are not associated with the end of life's happiness. For Sara, who sees her personal calling in geriatric care, this means "preserving the ability of the elderly to live an engaged and fulfilling life." For Brian, his vision is a younger generation that's even more active in the community than his peer group, allowing him to continue to advocate for those less fortunate with the knowledge that his work will continue on.

This vision statement isn't set in stone. It's a draft. So just write something. If it makes you want to rush out and take action, you're on the right track. Your vision statement should be inspiring to you. If it's not, try again.

My vision statement:

_____

_____

_____

_____

Once you're happy with your vision statement, write it down in your movie reel in Appendix B.

CHAPTER 8

Building Your Purpose

ELISSA ASHWOOD KNOWS WHAT IT'S LIKE to worry about the future. After making a name for herself as a business consultant and then building her own personal-strategy coaching firm, Truly Accomplished, she was diagnosed with breast cancer. I had lunch with her the day after she got the news. How would this impact her family? she wondered. How was she going to be able to grow her new business while undergoing chemotherapy? Elissa was certain that she was on the right track in her career and personal life; creating personal-management strategies for individuals and companies is her purpose. She just needed to figure out how to keep on going and crystallize her vision of the future.

"Humans aren't great at thinking very far ahead at all. Twenty years seems like infinity," she told me. "Not being able to think ahead is a problem because it means we tend to *overestimate* how much we can change things in the future that are really the sum of our actions over time—like our health. And we tend to *underestimate* how much time there really is for things like exploring interests, making mistakes, and learning."

So Elissa set a challenge for herself, one that I think is great for anyone considering their purpose and future: Using the steps in Exercise 8.1, live the next thirty years of your life. Think of it as hitting the fast-forward button on the movie of your life, and the DVD player is letting you jump ahead to different chapters.

EXERCISE 8.1

Your Future, Ten Years at a Time

Step 1. What is your life like now? Answer the following questions about your life today.

Today (Year 20____)

I am _____ years old.

My family members are

_____	Age: _____
_____	Age: _____
_____	Age: _____
_____	Age: _____
_____	Age: _____
_____	Age: _____

Where I live:

_____

What it's like:

_____

_____

What I do:

_____

_____

Step 2. Roll forward ten years into the future. Put yourself in that time *as if it is the present*. Really be there, and use details to help you picture what life will be like.

10 years from now (Year 20____)

I am _____ years old.

My family members are

	Age: _____
	Age: _____
	Age: _____
	Age: _____
	Age: _____
	Age: _____

Where I live:

_____

What it's like:

_____

_____

What I do:

_____

_____

Step 3. Move forward another ten years. Again, be detailed. Listing the people who are in your family and life helps you visualize what that future date will really be like.

20 years from now (Year 20_____)

I am _____ years old.

My family members are

_____ Age: _____

_____ Age: _____

_____ Age: _____

_____ Age: _____

_____ Age: _____

_____ Age: _____

Where I live:

_____

What it's like:

_____

_____

What I do:

_____

_____

Step 4. Keep pushing into the future for our last stage.

30 years from now (Year 20_____)
I am _____ years old.
My family members are

_____ Age: _____

_____ Age: _____

_____ Age: _____

_____ Age: _____

_____ Age: _____

_____ Age: _____

Where I live:

_____

What it's like:

_____

_____

What I do:

_____

_____

_____

You're now thirty years into the future, and there's no reason to stop there. If you want to keep rolling it forward five or ten years at a time, feel free to let your mind create your future. When you're finished, answer the following questions:

1. What did you learn about what's important to your future happiness?

_____

_____

_____

_____

2. What advice does your much older self have for you, such as about what to act on more or what to worry about less?

_____

_____

_____

_____

3. What does this inspire you to do right now?

_____

_____

_____

_____

4. What hints does this give you about what your vision and purpose might be?

_____

_____

_____

_____

_____

You have brains in your head. You have feet in your shoes.
You can steer yourself in any direction you choose.
—Dr. Seuss

Advice from Your Future You

◎ A much older me would tell a younger me to focus more. The older me would also say to be careful of who I let into my life. —*Tianna*

◎ Achieve all you would like while you're young and remember that happiness and having a healthy relationship with your family and friends are the most important things. Don't sweat the small stuff! —*Ashley*

◎ Spend more time traveling! You jumped into the workforce so quickly that you never got to see as much of the world as you had hoped to see before you had children. Worry less about money and more about experiences. Don't give up on organizing and the movement for social justice, even though it may not help you buy that house. Keep being passionate about encouraging change within the community. —*Justin*

◎ Do the things you love now; don't put them off until later. Don't worry about what the future has in store for you. Live every day like it's your last, and you'll be happy. —*Brett*

◎ Don't worry, because things will work out. You're going to get old either way, so why spend time doing lame or uninteresting things? —*Bennett*

◎ I should enjoy my loved ones now, while I still have the time. Be kind and forgiving. —*Jessica*

◎ Take chances! Do not be afraid of the little things. Worrying about stuff that might happen is really not worth the effort. Your parents will always be proud. Just follow your dreams, and you will be happy. If you get a job you love, you won't work a day in your life. —*Bob*

◎ My older self just told me what I really value: a good home, a strong family, a good career, and a good education. I realize now that everything I want for myself in the future is similar to everything I grew up with. And I need to go after it now! —*Audrey*

◎ Follow your dreams, no matter how big. And don't worry about the little things. Outward appearances aren't nearly as what's important on the inside and who you are as a person. —*Carolanne*

For most testers, this exercise highlighted the importance of family. For men and women alike it was an eye-opener that people and relationships ultimately matter much more than awards and accolades.

Mary felt inspired to spend more time with her grandparents after completing this exercise. "My grandma is eighty-three years old and gets sick all the time. She basically raised me and was a huge part of my life. I need to spend as much time with her as I possibly can while she is still here."

Kylee, a pharmacy student, said that thinking ahead into her future inspired her to get involved with different clubs and organizations that would help her fight against life-threatening diseases. "I just need to put the time and effort into it. I can start now on making my dreams come true. I don't have to be a pharmacist before I can start helping others."

▓ YOUR PURPOSE STATEMENT

Your *purpose* is the commitment to do something that lights you up inside while setting the world on fire. Your purpose will be focused on action; have a positive impact on others; use your talents, skills, and personal qualities; drive your short-term life and career goals; and make you want to get out of bed in the morning.

Review your vision statement from page 113. Your purpose is what you will do to live out your vision. Through your purpose, you use your talents, skills, and strengths to accomplish goals in service of your broader hope for change. Look back at the work you've done so far. What roles do you have to play in serving your vision?

here are too many ideas and things and people, too many directions to go. The reason it matters to care passionately about something is that it whittles the world down to a more manageable size.

—ADAPTATION (2002)

Ideally, your purpose is some-thing that will come through in all elements of your life—not only in your work life, but in your personal, physical, spiritual, and social life. Determining your purpose is a big task, and your purpose statement won't be cast in stone. That's fine.

But remember, for young adults, this book is about developing a *purpose* mindset and living *purpose-fully*. So don't feel constrained. Pick something that you are passionate about now—something that really speaks to your values and vision—and immerse yourself in it for a while. Changing your mind later is always an option.

EXERCISE 8.2

Drafting Your Purpose Statement

This exercise is adapted from several online and print sources aimed at helping us turn potentially scary and huge exercises into bite-sized pieces. If you're familiar with Mad Libs, you'll quickly grasp how it works.

Step 1. Identify a few action verbs that motivate you. Action verbs are things that you want to do—your passions. Look back at Exercise 6.2 and find your passions list. You can use the short list below to start you off. Thinking about your action verbs for life is a good way to help you crystallize your purpose and your vision for change.

Connect	Multiply	Rehabilitate
Explain	Organize	Strengthen
Gather	Preach	Synthesize
Grow	Protect	Teach
Maintain	Publicize	Translate

My life action verbs are:

_____   _____

_____   _____

_____   _____

Step 2. Review your core values from chapter 5 and look at the core values listed in your movie reel. Which core values excite, impassion, or drive you enough to take action?

_____   _____

_____   _____

_____   _____

My core values are:

_____   _____

_____   _____

_____   _____

Step 3. Whom do you want to serve, impact, or otherwise help? To what cause or audience are you willing to devote your passion and time, and your unique blend of talents, skills, interests, and values? Whom do you want to be around? Whom do you want to learn from? Whom do you want to impact in a positive way? Look back at previous chapters for refreshers on your earlier answers, or use this short list as a way to spark ideas.

Animals	Friends	Natural disaster areas	Spiritual or religious group
Children	Global relations		
Clients		Personal growth	War zones
Community	Local commerce	The planet	Work
Country			
Family	The marginalized	Race and gender issues	

I would like to serve, help, or impact:

_____

_____

_____

The way you get meaning in your life is to devote yourself to loving others,
devote yourself to your community around you, and devote yourself to
creating something that gives you purpose and meaning.

—MITCH ALBOM, AUTHOR

Step 4. Put it all together. By combining your action verbs, values, and impact groups into one sentence, you'll get a first draft of a purpose statement.

Try this fill-in-the-blanks exercise, using some of the words you just wrote down. Feel free to adapt the wording a bit here and there to meet your needs. If it doesn't make grammatical sense, don't get too hung up on that. Instead, the idea is to see how these ideas can interact, and then to craft (or recraft) a purpose and vision statement that feels right to you.

Follow this model:

My purpose is to _____ , _____ , and _____
                      (action verb)   (action verb)   (action verb)

so that I can live my values of _____ , _____ , and _____
                                   (value)   (value)   (value)

to make a difference by impacting _____ .
                                        (imapct group)

Write yours here:

_____

_____

_____

Sit with that fill-in-the-blanks sentence for a bit. Remember, purpose and meaning come from connecting to something that is bigger than you—and from pursuing goals that are valuable and important toward achieving that end. Think about how you might want to focus, broaden, or improve your fill-in-the-blanks purpose statement to create a true representation of your purpose today, and as time goes on. You can adjust your purpose statement as your life stages change.

Purpose in Action

To be a loud voice for fairness, equality, and justice. —Jackson

To use my skills to become a physical therapist, so that I can help people grow physically and emotionally. —Alyssa

To help solve the financial crisis so that future generations don't have to go through what we are going through now. I will use my education and skills to educate our leaders so that we can move into a more prosperous financial future. —Bob

To do everything in my power to help students who are bullied by being there for them when everyone else turns their backs because of stupid rumors. Things really do get better. —Jessica

Explore what makes people and ideas one-in-a-million so that I can connect teaching and empowering youth to reimagine the world's problems and generate new solutions. —Bennett

◼ YOUR EPITAPH

The following exercise can ensure that you are on the path toward living your purpose and not getting distracted by short-term goals along the way. But get ready: it's pretty dark. Give yourself some space to do this one, and if this exercise is too much or makes you feel uncomfortable, just read through it for now and come back to it when you're ready.

The *tombstone technique* is adapted from Matthew McKay and colleague's *Your Life on Purpose*, a thoroughly researched book written by three psychologists specializing in acceptance and commitment therapy. With this approach, you'll be writing a single sentence that sums up what your life was about. This sentence ideally should capture what matters—or mattered—to you most. It's the crystallization of your vision and purpose.

EXERCISE 8.3

The Tombstone Technique

Step 1. Fast-forward into the future. You've recently died, and your tombstone is being engraved. On it is your name and the phrase "A person who . . ."

Close your eyes. Focus on your breathing a bit, or do whatever you need to do to slow yourself down.

Step 2. Take a moment to think, and then write down your sentence in the tombstone space on the next page. It might take a draft or two, so work on it until you're satisfied.

"This is your life, the core of what you're here to do," writes psychologist Matthew McKay, lead author of *Your Life on Purpose*. "Look at the words and let them settle inside of you. Feel them in your heart and in your gut. Now, ask yourself this question: 'How close or far am I from what I want my life to be about?' Notice what comes up."

A PERSON WHO

This is your opportunity to decide to move in the direction you want to take and to embrace your life of purpose. In the next chapter you'll make purpose-based commitments to get there, but for now, just sit with the big picture: Is this who I want to be? Am I living this life now?

Once you are satisfied with your purpose, reviewing both your purpose statement and your tombstone epitaph, add it to your movie reel in Appendix B. "As the star and producer of the movie of his/her life, _____ is a person who . . ."

CHAPTER 9

Committed to Purpose

IN HIS 2015 DARTMOUTH COLLEGE COMMENCEMENT ADDRESS, *New York Times* columnist and author David Brooks tackled the challenges of commitment head on: "We are not a society that nurtures commitment-making," he said. "We live in a culture that puts a lot of emphasis on individual liberty and freedom of choice. . . . Student culture is built around keeping your options open and fear of missing out." Our phones are always enticing us to shift our attention span, he said, and if you can't focus your attention for thirty seconds, how can you make a commitment for life?

The paradox, he said, is that your fulfillment in life "will not come from how well you explore your freedom and keep your options open. That's the path to a frazzled, scattered life in which you try to please everyone and end up pleasing no one." Instead, your fulfillment in life will come "by how well you end your freedom." Brooks told the graduates, "By the time you hit your thirties, you will realize that your primary mission in life is to be really good at making commitments."

Commitments can be scary, but they don't have to be. Brooks describes commitments as "falling in love with something, and then building a structure of behavior around it that will carry you through when your love falters. When you make a commitment to something you truly love, whether it's a spouse, a job, a company, or a school, it won't feel like you are putting on an uncomfortable lobster shell. It will feel like you are taking off the shell and becoming the shape you were meant to be."

Commitments are the engines that drive a purposeful life. Working toward your vision for change and living your purpose mean making the choice to shape your life and become someone: to do something and commit to the crazy ride of life. It's turning your life into kinetic energy. But to do so, you need to make choices and forsake the limitless possibilities to focus on a few.

Theologian Thomas Aquinas spoke in the language of first and second freedoms: First freedoms are a state of potential, with lots of choices, and second freedoms are about making choices, and commitments, and living a life of purpose. The transition from adolescence to adulthood is the transition from first freedoms to second freedoms, from potential energy to kinetic energy, and from fuzzy vision to committed purpose.

Understand, though, that this transition is often challenging, because wanting something is not the same as committing to it. Desire is not the same as action. This is where most self-help and behavioral-change programs fail: Finding your purpose is admirable, but are you committed to living it?

When you are inspired by some great purpose, some extraordinary project, all your thoughts break their bonds: Your mind transcends limitations, your consciousness expands in every direction, and you find yourself in a new, great, and wonderful world. Dormant forces, faculties, and talents become alive, and you discover yourself to be a greater person by far than you ever dreamed yourself to be.

—PATANJALI, INDIAN AUTHOR

You've identified your talents, skills, and strengths. You've crystallized your vision for change. *Now it's time to make purpose-based commitments and create specific purpose-based goals so that you can begin to take concrete steps toward realizing your vision and living in a purposeful way.*

Here's the sad truth: We're really good at doing what we feel like doing, but we're not always great at doing what we said we'd do. Commitment problems aren't just about human relations. We've all got problems with commitment because it's not something we practice all that often.

Making a commitment to living your purpose means being aware of your *values* and your *vision*. Take a look back to chapter 5 and remind yourself of your core values. Are you ready to live them on a daily basis? Do they speak to the purpose statement you've drafted? Then remind yourself of your vision. Is that cause or dream worth working toward, worth giving up some of those other possibilities so that you can devote yourself more completely to achieving it?

I hope you've answered with a resounding *yes*. If not, go back and rethink those values and vision exercises until you are sure that you're excited to live them. Once you're motivated to turn wanting into doing, make purpose-based commitments that turn your broader vision into achievable goals in all aspects of your life.

Ask yourself, "As I live my values and work toward achieving my vision, what do I know I want to see as aspects of my life?"

> *Efforts and courage are not enough without purpose and direction.*
> —JOHN F. KENNEDY, US PRESIDENT

For example, in the *work* category, Ellie said that, keeping in mind her values of financial stability and excitement, and her vision of educating all children regardless of economic background, she would make the following commitments toward her purpose of starting a nonprofit to fund disadvantaged schools:

- ▶ I will earn $50,000 per year or more, so that I can save at least 15 percent annually toward my future charity.
- ▶ I will use my problem-solving skills each day.
- ▶ I will do work that allows me to live in a big city.

Angie made the following purpose-based commitments about her *relationships*, keeping in mind her number-one value of personal integrity and her vision of a large, thriving family life:

▶   I will be appreciated for my personality and temperament. I will not
     have to pretend to be a different person or play by others' rules for
     relationships.
  ▶ I will use my sense of humor to make time for silly fun each day.
  ▶ No more dead-end relationships; either I think he could be the one, or
     I'll end it.

For the *community* category, Jonathan listed his purpose-based commitments
acknowledging his values of creating beauty and environmental sustainability, and
his vision for inspiring an urban-garden movement in population-dense cities:
  ▶ I will preserve natural beauty, bringing green spaces to as many neigh-
     borhoods as I can.
  ▶ No more academic degrees. I'll take a few courses if necessary, but
     mostly I want to be about *doing*.
  ▶ I will involve local residents in all my community-based projects.

For Mitchell, whose purpose is to increase awareness about bigotry and preju-
dice to move toward a vision of a more tolerant society, he identified his guiding
value in the *free-time* category as the ability to enjoy life. His vision is to spend more
time with family and friends, and to do meaningful fun things. To achieve this, his
purpose-based commitments in this area are to:
  ▶ Be at home with my wife and kids a good amount of time.
  ▶ Invite friends and relatives over to the house.
  ▶ Go on vacations or trips as much as possible.

EXERCISE 9.1

Purpose-Based Commitments

Now it is your turn. Consider those eight big aspects of your life. Thinking about your values and vision, what purpose-based commitments do you want to make in each area?

Family	Education	Work	Physical
Financial	Spiritual	Relationships	Free time

Note: *If one of these areas doesn't apply to you, add an area of your own. Feel free to customize the exercise to best meet your needs.*

Family

Guiding value:_____

Guiding vision:_____

Purpose-based commitments: _____

1. _____

2. _____

3. _____

Education

Guiding value:_____

Guiding vision:_____

Purpose-based commitments: _____

1. _____

2. _____

3. _____

Work

Guiding value:_____

Guiding vision:_____

Purpose-based commitments:_____

1._____

2._____

3._____

Physical

Guiding value:_____

Guiding vision:_____

Purpose-based commitments:_____

1._____

2._____

3._____

Financial

Guiding value:_____

Guiding vision:_____

Purpose-based commitments:_____

1._____

2._____

3._____

Spiritual

Guiding value: _____

Guiding vision: _____

Purpose-based commitments: _____

1. _____

2. _____

3. _____

Relationships

Guiding value: _____

Guiding vision: _____

Purpose-based commitments: _____

1. _____

2. _____

3. _____

Free Time

Guiding value: _____

Guiding vision: _____

Purpose-based commitments: _____

1. _____

2. _____

3. _____

Once you are satisfied with your purpose-based commitments, write the top commitment in each category into your movie reel in Appendix B.

Purpose and Peace

Q: Have you thought about questions of purpose or calling before? If so, in what context?

A: By myself? Yes. With friends? Sometimes. For years I struggled to find a passion and purpose. It's probably normal, though. When I graduated high school—an average student—I thought I was destined to work in investment banking. I quickly realized that I derived great energy from being there for others. Now more than ever, as I enter into a counseling psychology doctoral program, I recognize how incredible it is to be following my passion. I've shared it with all my close friends. . . . I feel peace.

—SAM

▪ REWARDS

Commitment to a goal isn't costless. Your choices have consequences, so choose to commit yourself to something that you really want to do, not something that you feel you should do or that your parents want you to do. Review your list and disregard anything that seems like a *should* rather than a value-based commitment. To make sure that your commitments are right for you, Exercise 9.2 can help you identify your true rewards.

No matter how altruistic we try to be while living our purpose and making commitments to fulfill an outward-centered vision, being appreciated and rewarded feels good. Indeed, studies have found that young adults would rather receive a compliment than eat their favorite food. But not all compliments and rewards are created equal. If I told you that I'd give you a $50 Starbucks gift card if you lived out your purpose for a year, you'd probably give me a quizzical look. While lattes are tasty, research finds that extrinsic (external) rewards of things don't usually provide the long-term, meaningful motivation we need to live out deep commitments to vision and purpose. *Rewards are more meaningful when they are intrinsic—coming from within you—and if they are in line with your values and purpose.* When acknowledging the good you do for others, your community, and the world—rather than simply doing something that feels good for a short time—those kinds of rewards really make an impact.

Take a minute to think about the rewards that are meaningful to you: Do you want to leave a legacy? To be acknowledged and appreciated by large groups of people? Are you looking for the opportunity to dress up? To be the go-to person or the big boss? To have control over your schedule? To feel financially secure?

As you brainstorm, think about whether the reward is attached to one of your core values or is recognition for a talent, skill, or strength that will help you live your outward-focused purpose. These rewards are the ones that will give you the most long-lasting satisfaction.

I don't provide a list with Exercise 9.2 because I want you to brainstorm what's important to you as an individual. Being honest is crucial here. This list is personal, and yours shouldn't look like anyone else's.

Sometimes rewards might seem random to others but essential to you. For example, I realized for me the importance that my research be good cocktail-party conversation. While that sounds a bit silly, the reward speaks to my core value of educating others and my vision of translating academic research so that it can have a real impact on someone's everyday life. Having people excited to talk to me about my research is a meaningful reward.

As some examples, for Alyssa, being financially secure is an important reward she seeks. The values attached to that reward are to be responsible with the money she earns and make good financial decisions. For Samantha, being loved and valued is a reward she seeks, and because of that, she values healthy relationships with family, friends, and her community.

EXERCISE 9.2

Find Your True Rewards

With your vision and purpose in mind, make a list of rewards that mean something to you, as well as the values that are attached to that reward.

Reward I Seek: _____

Value(s) Attached to That Reward: _____

_____

Reward I Seek: _____

Value(s) Attached to That Reward: _____

_____

Reward I Seek: _____

Value(s) Attached to That Reward: _____

_____

Reward I Seek: _____

Value(s) Attached to That Reward: _____

_____

Reward I Seek: _____

Value(s) Attached to That Reward: _____

_____

▨ COMMITMENTS

Go back and look at your big list of purpose-based commitments from Exercise 9.1. To prioritize your commitments, think of which ones really speak to the true rewards you need for personal fulfillment. Keeping commitments takes a lot of energy, and you need all the rewards and reinforcement you can get along the way.

Why should you prioritize your commitments? Consider the perpetual case of the broken New Year's resolutions.

It's January 1, and you've created a list of New Year's resolutions. In the fog of the morning, you look at this list—commitments to lose weight, organize your closet, save money, and so on—and you feel great about your goals. A new beginning. Right?

Fast-forward to mid-February. If your resolutions have held up, you're in the minority. Every year, millions of people make New Year's resolutions, and many reports show that more than 75 percent of them fail. We roll our eyes when we hear politicians promise, "This will be a top priority for my administration"—on everything from potholes to job creation—because we know that not everything can be a top priority. But somehow we think our lofty list of personal goals is different.

It's laudable to want to shed those extra pounds and get into better shape. Organizing your closet and giving extra clothes to Goodwill is an excellent idea. Of course, saving more money will help you in many aspects of your life. But trying to do a handful of new things all at once, researchers find, is a recipe for failure.

Exerting self-control takes energy. In their book *Willpower: Rediscovering the Greatest Human Strength*, Roy Baumeister and John Tierney point to dozens of studies to show that when we are asked to exert self-control in one area, we are less able to focus and exert control in another area. In a study that Baumeister and his team conducted in 1998, undergraduates were asked to fast for several hours and then were brought into a room that smelled of fresh-baked chocolate chip cookies. On the table were a plate of warm cookies, a plate of chocolate, and a plate of radishes. Some of the students were invited to eat the cookies and chocolate, while others were told that they were welcome only to the radishes. The researchers left the room but secretly watched to see what happened.

The radish people struggled to resist the cookies and chocolate. They gazed longingly at the treats; some even picked up the cookies and smelled them. But no one broke the rules; everyone in the radish condition, as the nomenclature goes, managed to resist the temptation to eat the cookies or chocolates. Then all the students were brought in to do geometry puzzles. Of course, the students thought it was a test of intelligence, but the researchers made the puzzles insolvable. The goal was to see how long the students would try to solve the puzzles before giving up.

The students who had been allowed to eat the cookies and chocolates persisted in trying to solve the puzzles for more than twice as long as those who had been in the radish condition. Those who had to resist the cookies and chocolates lasted just eight minutes on the puzzle, while those who ate the cookies or chocolates lasted about twenty minutes.

Exerting the willpower to resist the treats took energy. The hungry students who had resisted the cookies used up their self-control and had very little left for the geometry puzzle. This clever experiment sums up the temptations we face every day and gives us a clue as to why sometimes we're able to resist and sometimes we're not.

If you've taken the time to fill out the list of purpose-based commitments in each life category—commitments that speak to your values and your vision—you have a dauntingly long list. This long list, though, is a good and necessary thing. You want to make sure that you have commitments to live out your values in all areas of your life. But it's going to be hard to do them all at once.

EXERCISE 9.3

Prioritize Your Commitments

Look back at your list of purpose-based commitments on page 135 and see which ones really speak to the true rewards you are craving right now. Make a top-five list of commitments. They should come from several areas of your life, so that you are balanced in your focus and commitments. These are commitments you are making to yourself about how you want your life to be as you work toward your vision and your purpose. But these are still big-picture ideas.

My Top-Five Purpose-Based Commitments

1. _____

2. _____

3. _____

4. _____

5. _____

■ FORMULATING ACHIEVABLE GOALS

Making these top-five purpose-based commitments a reality—in your life or in the life of your community—requires clear goals. Goals are stepping-stones that keep you on track as you live your purpose. They are essential for monitoring progress, rewarding it, and determining next steps.

Goals are dreams with deadlines.
—DIANA SCHARF HUNT, AUTHOR

Ellie has a vision of educating all children equally, regardless of economic background. Her purpose, she feels, is to create and manage a thriving nonprofit to fund disadvantaged schools, and she made purpose-based commitments to earn $50,000 per year or more, so that she could save at least 15 percent annually toward her future charity; to use her problem-solving skills each day; and to do work that allows her to live in a big city.

Looking at her first purpose-based commitment, she set the following short- and medium-term goals to turn her commitment into action:

Purpose-Based Commitment 1: Earn $50,000 per year or more so that I can save at least 15 percent annually toward my future charity.

Goals:
▶ Research jobs at finance firms that have a nonprofit arm.
▶ Do at least two informational interviews to see what summer jobs, classes, etc., I need on my resume to help get this kind of job.
▶ Create a budget to see whether I can actually save 15 percent and live comfortably in the city where these finance firms are based.

Bob wants to make more time for his family. He is committing to that by setting a goal of visiting his grandparents and parents each week. Brett listed planning—for the good things and bad things that come along—as a purpose-based commitment. Financially, he's set goals to seek advice from money-management experts, invest in smart purchases rather than impulse buys, and create a budget so he knows where he stands.

> "*I*f the sky were to suddenly open up, there would be no law, there would be no rule. There would be only you and your memories, the choices you've made and the people you've touched."
> —DONNIE DARKO (2001)

EXERCISE 9.4

Turning Purpose-Based Commitments into Achievable Goals

Look at your purpose-based commitments and write out your short-term and medium-term goals to turn these into realities. Set yourself up for success: Think about goals that are both meaningful and achievable.

Purpose-Based Commitment #1: _____

_____

Goals to make that commitment a reality:

1. _____

2. _____

3. _____

Purpose-Based Commitment #2: _____

_____

Goals to make that commitment a reality:

1. _____

2. _____

3. _____

Purpose-Based Commitment #3: _____

_____

Goals to make that commitment a reality:

1. _____

2. _____

3. _____

Purpose-Based Commitment #4: _____

_____

Goals to make that commitment a reality:

1. _____

2. _____

3. _____

Purpose-Based Commitment #5: _____

_____

Goals to make that commitment a reality:

1. _____

2. _____

3. _____

The students who worked through this book in its beta version said that this was the hardest—but most rewarding—section of the book. It's the time you go from exploring to choosing a path, from possibilities to commitments to action. And yes, it's challenging.

If you skipped over any exercises in this section, consider pausing here until you have some time to complete them. It's through the completion of these exercises—and following through on your commitments—that you embrace purposeful living in your life. Not next year, not when you're old. Today.

Research shows that writing down your commitments helps you achieve them.

But there are two other crucial steps to creating this documentary of your purposeful life: identifying potential plot twists and surrounding yourself with a great supporting cast.

The next section will help you anticipate what might get in the way, what might throw you off course, and what challenges you might face in your purpose journey.

It will also help you ask the right questions to find mentors and support systems to make your life documentary as meaningful as possible.

Part 3
Bringing
Purpose to Life

CHAPTER 10

Plot Twists

WHEN WE HEAR STORIES ABOUT FAMOUS PEOPLE, we just get the sizzle reel—the highlights that capture their rise to stardom in a few quick sound bites. In our own lives, that's often the case, too: From social media to annual holiday cards, the good stuff gets the airtime. You post the most flattering photos, the pithiest comments, and the biggest accomplishments.

But life isn't lived in a sizzle reel of highlights. It doesn't unfold in a straight line. Neither does a captivating movie. There are plot twists in your life that throw you off course and fears that hold you back.

By now, you've identified your vision statement and made commitments and specific goals toward living your purpose. You're in a prime position to start affecting change in your own life and the lives of others. But this isn't always going to be an easy journey.

Since you're the producer of your own movie in addition to being the star, you need to take steps to identify and overcome obstacles that come from within, from the challenges of conflicting choices, and even from friends. All of these new inputs will trigger feelings, some of which may make you feel uncomfortable and doubtful about your abilities to succeed in your goals, your purpose, and your vision.

Feelings, though, are fickle, and they are a weak choice for our foundations and actions. Too often, the things we care most about are replaced by things that merely comfort us. And just because you're willing to live purposefully doesn't keep you from having thoughts and feelings that run counter to your values or get in your way, note Matthew McKay and his coauthors in their book *Your Life on Purpose*. Thinking about your vision and purpose—and the commitments you'll make to live them—means that, on a deeper level, you know you're committed to staying on course, and you do it for a meaningful reason: the underlying value and vision matter to you more than the obstacles that stand in your way.

In this chapter I ask you to anticipate—and think about how you'll overcome—some of the biggest plot twists you'll face as you live a meaningful and purposeful life. These obstacles will come from life facts (Plot Twist 1 on how to pay the bills while living purposefully), from inside of you (Plot Twist 2 on the runaway mind), from external sources (Plot Twist 3 on the peanut gallery), and from the general pressures of life (Plot Twist 4 on conflicting choices). Anticipating problems is a key step to keep you on track to achieve your goals and work toward your purpose, whatever it is.

■ PLOT TWIST 1: PAYING FOR YOUR PURPOSE

"Purpose is a luxury. It's for rich, older people who can afford to think about meaning," Annie said to me over coffee in the early days of my research. "I have thousands of dollars in student loans. I want to do something meaningful, but I've got to pay the bills."

This is one of the most common myths about purpose—that it's for someone else, sometime later, but not for me and not now. But purpose isn't constrained to one type of job or even jobs at all. It's not just for folks who have prestigious careers or who are directly helping people on a day-to-day basis. It's for you, right now, as you've seen in the preceding chapters. You don't have to win the lottery, or get older. The time is now: The sooner you start living with a purpose mindset, the happier and more fulfilled you will be.

The vast majority of college students will graduate with student loan debt. On average, college students are buried under about $30,000 in loans. Credit card debt digs an even deeper ditch for many others, and graduate school may compound the financial problems.

It's all fine and good to give the "follow your passions" advice, but when you have $10 in your checking account, what you need is a *job*. You have two ways to look at that job: as a stopgap measure that is just paying the bills, or as an opportunity to live purposefully—regardless of what the job entails.

"It's considered a really negative thing to say you're just getting a job to have a job," says Jen, a senior. "Even worse, there are only a few kinds of jobs that are acceptable. If you're graduating from college and you decide that your purpose is to serve others as a grocery-store cashier, you feel like you're not allowed to do that.

"There's this pressure to do at least one better than your parents' generation," she continued. "Maybe it's a fear of being left behind, but really it's like society defines purpose as achievement—and usually measures success in dollars and net worth—so there's pressure to achieve in a really restrictive way."

Do Jen's concerns tap into any of the pressures you feel right now?

"*D*on't ever let somebody tell you you can't do something, not even me. All right? Your dream, you gotta protect it. People can't do something themselves, they wanna tell you you can't do it. If you want something, go get it. Period."
—THE PURSUIT OF HAPPYNESS (2006)

EXERCISE 10.1

Pressure to Find a Paying Purpose

Consider these questions, and take some time to answer one or all of them in as much detail as you can.

1. Do you feel pressure to find a paying job that ties into your life purpose? If so, where does that pressure come from? Is the expectation reasonable, or can you be happy separating your purpose from paid employment—instead living your purpose, for example, through family life, community service, or an unpaid hobby?

2. Do you feel pressure to find a certain kind of job? What kinds of jobs are acceptable and what kinds are unacceptable? Where does this pressure come from? If you were released from this kind of pressure, what kind of job would you want to do?

_____

_____

_____

_____

_____

_____

_____

_____

_____

Jobs, Careers, and Callings

Aaron Hurst started a company called Taproot. It's a nonprofit organization that pairs up legal professionals with pro-bono jobs. If you were a lawyer and wanted to help people who couldn't afford legal services, Taproot would match you with someone who could use your legal expertise, and you'd do it for free, as volunteer work.

Aaron was fascinated that people said the work they did for free felt so much more meaningful than the work they did for pay . . . even if it was the exact same work. He realized that most people think purposeful work has to be volunteer work—that to find meaning in your work, you have to find your cause. So often, that's what we set out to do—helping the homeless, saving animals or the environment, or helping children, as examples.

But purpose isn't something that only comes with particular jobs. Nor is it only for the educated, rich, privileged, or older person. Moreover, participating in causes doesn't always lead to a sense of meaning anyway.

Aaron's investigations led him to write a book called *The Purpose Economy*, in which he argued that purpose isn't a cause, revelation, or a luxury. It's a choice.

Purpose is something you *do* on a daily basis, and living with a purpose mindset is something you can *do* right now.

Purpose is all about how you approach your work.

You may have heard the parable about three stonemasons who were laying bricks. A man walked up and asked what they were doing. "I'm laying bricks," said the first. The second said, "I'm building a wall." And the third said, "I'm building a cathedral." All three share the same day-to-day labor, but they have different perspectives. Some people see their work as a specific function, some as part of a larger project, and some as a calling.

Yale professor Amy Wrzesniewski researches the difference among these attitudes, finding that people with callings—the cathedral builders—view their work in ways that allow them to experience it as a source of joy and meaning.

You can go from viewing your work as a job to seeing your purposeful calling by "crafting" your job into something that uses your strengths and skills, and by fostering connections with your colleagues. The idea is to focus on what your job could be, rather than become stuck in the rut of what you think it currently is.

For example, if you have a part-time job while you're in school, think about how you are spending your work time. Are you fixating on the stuff you can't do particularly well? Procrastinating until it's too late? Not everything is going to be fun, but focusing on the tasks at which you excel gives you the strength to navigate through the ones you don't like.

Ask yourself, too: *How does my work impact others?* Every job touches the life of someone else. It's a matter of choosing to see your work as meaningful.

Spending

If you want to live with purpose, spend with purpose. The choices you make about how you use your (limited) resources can have a major impact on your ability to thrive now and in the future.

We often accumulate stuff because we're spending without thinking about our larger purpose. If you want to stop accumulating stuff, start figuring out your values.

EXERCISE 10.2

Spending Purposefully

Look back at your core values in chapter 5 and your movie reeel in Appendix B to figure out what financial means you'd need to achieve them. Be as specific as possible.

My core values are   To have the means to achieve them, I need to

_____   _____

_____   _____

_____   _____

_____   _____

_____   _____

As an example, here's the list Ashley made for herself:

My core values are	To have the means to achieve them, I need to
Balance	Cut back my "play money" from $45 to $20 per month by not buying soda, coffee, etc. on the run
Security	Put half my paycheck into savings each month
Happiness	Spend my "play money" on things that make me really happy, not necessities
Peace of mind	Create a logbook of savings and plan repayment of loans
Love/relationships	Set aside $10 every two weeks to treat my boyfriend or roommate to dinner, ice cream, or a movie

Your friends, family, and work or school colleagues all give you a sense of what normal is for your peer group, and what you should or should not be buying or doing. But those cues don't necessarily add up to your own values. Take a few minutes to try to separate your values from everyone else's to help you spend a bit more purposefully. You might ask yourself the following questions:

▶ What kind of car do you think you should be driving based on your social cues? How important is your car to your core values?

▶ What kind of clothes should a person of your social or employment status be wearing? How important is fashion to those core goals?

▶ What kind of shampoo do you think someone like you should have in the bathroom? How important is that to you?

Distinguishing what you yourself actually value from the surrounding culture's values is a positive first step to cutting down unnecessary spending.

What If My Purpose and My Job Aren't the Same Thing?

Living purposefully doesn't mean that every moment of your life has to be focused around some singular idea of purpose. While in an ideal world your paid work would fill you with meaning and purpose, sometimes doing work that you don't love—but doing it well, with pride, and in service of some larger goal—is very purposeful.

José's father was employed in a factory. He worked hard each day and then came home to his family. Once at home, he took his sons to their baseball games, and he worked in the garage after the kids went to sleep, tinkering and building things. José's mother and father saved enough money to pay part of the way so that José and his younger brother could go to college. José was the first in the family to graduate from college.

"Was my father's purpose to work at a factory? No. His passion was as an inventor. He'd create all sorts of things in the garage. If something broke, he'd fix it. He'd spend hours fixing a three-dollar toy, because he loved that sort of stuff," said José. "But should my dad have quit the factory job and spent his life in the garage building stuff? I don't think that would have been more purposeful. His purpose was to provide for us. And he did that with pride. He's a role model for me in purpose, not because of his job, but because of his commitment to us."

Look back at the commitments you've made—and to whom you've made them. What do you need to do to uphold those commitments?

As David Brooks told Dartmouth graduates in his 2015 commencement address, a commitment is a moral act.

> The moral world is not structured like the market world. It has an inverse logic. To develop morally and inside you have to follow an inverse set of

rules. You have to give to receive. You have to surrender to something outside yourself to gain strength within yourself. You have to conquer your desire to get what you crave. Success leads to the greatest failure, which is arrogance and pride. Failure can lead to the greatest success, which is humility and learning. In order to fulfill yourself, you have to forget yourself. In order to find yourself, you have to lose yourself.

Taking a job is not a moral act, he said. Having a vocation is a moral act. Making a commitment is a moral act. Becoming a good, moral person isn't about individual character as much as the ability to make commitments.

▌PLOT TWIST 2: THE RUNAWAY MIND

Among the biggest obstacles you'll face as you work toward change and live your purpose is fear. Fear of failure, fear of being alone, fear of being ridiculed—you name it, fears hold us back. Our minds take a fear and just run wild with it.

As a general rule, you probably try to avoid things that you fear. But you've also heard all those lessons about why it's important to face your fears if you want to achieve something important. Why? "Fear is a sign that you are entering a personal frontier," explains Barbara Braham in *Finding Your Purpose: A Guide to Personal Fulfillment*. Fear is a sign that you are taking a risk and you are likely to feel fear "at the moment when you are about to stretch yourself to new growth."

> *Let's not forget that the little emotions are the great captains of our lives, and we obey them without realizing it.*
> —VINCENT VAN GOGH, ARTIST

What do you fear most? This question makes us uncomfortable because we often try not to think about the things we fear. Yet by not acknowledging our fears, we often let them run our lives—and keep us from living our purpose—without ever knowing about it. As actress and author Jamie Lee Curtis is quoted as saying, "Everything you want in the world is just right outside your comfort zone . . . every single thing you could possibly want."

EXERCISE 10.3

Your Greatest Fears

What do you fear the most? Here's a list for starters, but feel free to add your own.

Authority	Failure	Never being content
Being alone	Illness and pain	Not being successful
Being invisible	Looking dumb	Not belonging anywhere
Being ridiculed	Making a mistake	Not finding a job
Being trapped	Making the wrong decision	Poverty
Death		Public speaking
Disappointing people	Meeting new people	Other

My fears also include:

_____

_____

_____

_____

_____

As you look over your list of fears, would any in particular keep you from living out your purpose more fully?

I discovered that people are not really afraid of dying; they're afraid of not having ever lived, not ever having deeply considered their life's higher purpose, and not ever having stepped into that purpose and at least tried to make a difference in this world.

—JOSEPH JAWORSKI, AUTHOR

For Rachel, a production assistant in Los Angeles, her fear was that she was sacrificing too much to live her dream of working in movies. Rachel lives far away from her family and works unpredictable hours.

> Sometimes I fear that pursuing my calling is keeping me from a life I always thought I would have.
>
> I'd be lying if I didn't say I often feel torn between wanting to be in two different worlds. I have had to move away from my family, which has been the biggest sacrifice by far. I am a homebody, and family is one of the most important things to me. I would venture to say that if I didn't have a sense of calling to work in the film industry, I would have left it a long time ago. I have also had to watch all of my friends go on to get married and have kids without me. In high school and even in college, I never thought I would be where I am right now. It's both very good and very difficult at the same time.

Faith guides Rachel through the tough times and has helped her overcome these fears and doubts. "I keep pushing because I believe I'm doing what God wants me to be doing right now and when things seem impossible, I trust that he will use me in ways I can't see."

Focusing on the individual benefits of her work also helps tame her runaway mind, and Rachel sees her Hollywood experience on a micro level. "If I can make my boss a happier person (or the other people I work with) then he, in turn, will be more likely to make a positive impact on the people around him."

Her purpose-based career also matches her talents and skills—an excellent indication that Rachel is on the right path. "It's true what they say when it comes to getting a good job in the film industry: A lot of it is being in the right place at the right time. But you need to be good at your job to keep it," says Rachel. "To be a personal assistant you must be organized, thorough, have attention to detail, have good communication skills, and be a problem solver. In my experience, you also need to have common sense and an ability to disappear when you need to."

But there have been plenty of plot twists and challenges along the way: being a single woman who looks young for her age has made it difficult for Rachel to be taken seriously in a male-dominated industry. "Sometimes I doubt that my skin is thick enough to deal with all the crap. But at the same time I have an overwhelming sense that I'm where I am supposed to be at this point in my life.

"Never stop searching," says Rachel. "When you stop searching for your purpose is when the risk of losing sight of your purpose begins."

As you look through your list of fears, are there are a few that you might be able to quell—even a bit—by putting faith in yourself, your skills and talents, and the power of living your purpose?

EXERCISE 10.4

Overcoming Fears

▶ Which of my fears might I be able to overcome if I really believed I was on the right path?

▶ What would I need to know about myself—my skills, talents, interests, and vision—to push through these fears?

▶ Are any of these fears actually useful, such as in sending me valuable signals or information about the choices I should make in my future?

Jot down your notes and thoughts here:

_____

_____

Anxiety

One common manifestation of the runaway mind—so common it gets an exercise all of its own—is anxiety. In his book on helping young adults choose a career, *Pathfinder* author Nicholas Lore calls these the "yeah-buts." For example, you might say to yourself, *I want to start my own business*. Yeah, but *that's for people with a lot more money and experience than I have*," or "*I want to ask Alex out*. Yeah, that'd be great, but *I'm totally not cool enough for Alex to even consider dating me*.

"Every time you make a big stretch, a little voice inside your head tells you why you shouldn't do it, why it wouldn't work, why it is dangerous, why you should just keep doing what you were doing before you got these wild ideas," Lore writes. These yeah-buts often *sound like* the truth, and they can easily derail us from living our purpose unless we acknowledge and examine them.

Sam, the recent college graduate who became active in suicide prevention when one of his residential advisees committed suicide, says he constantly struggles with anxieties about whether he is lesser than or weaker than his stronger, smarter peers. "I constantly felt incompetent in comparison to these high-functioning students. But I was mentally struggling under the weight [of dealing with his personal grief]. For years, I was afraid to admit it—afraid to be perceived as weak. Sometimes, in the face of new suicides, the task felt too daunting to tackle. Sometimes I hesitated to bring up these hurts. I kept new ideas quiet for fear of rejection. This fear stifled progress and connectedness." By identifying his fears and anxieties, Sam has been able to continue on in his valuable work.

EXERCISE 10.5

Anxieties and Yeah-Buts

Check off any of these yeah-buts, adapted from Lore's work, that apply to you and add some more of your own as needed.

_____ I'm too young, too old, too smart, or not smart enough.

_____ I'll never get into the right school.

_____ I'm not a risk-taker.

_____ I'm not persuasive enough.

_____ My ideas aren't captivating enough.

_____ I'm not committed enough.

_____ It's just so difficult to decide what to do.

_____ I'm really trying. It's not my fault. Really!

_____ I don't have enough talent.

_____ I can't do what I want because the fun careers pay less.

_____ I want to help people, but this is a cruel, heartless world where only the lawyers win.

_____ It's all karma, so what's the point?

_____ I picked the wrong major.

_____ It takes too much work, and that's not my style.

_____ I should have been born earlier.

_____ I'm afraid, and that must be telling me something.

_____ I don't have enough money.

Add a few of your own:

_____

_____

_____

Don't believe everything you think.

—Bumper sticker

Monsters on the Bus

Abbey is anxious that she's picked a career path that might impact her ability to start a family, that she might not be living up to her potential, and that she will be paying off her student loans forever. These are all reasonable anxieties, but are they helping her say yes to opportunities or holding her back in fear?

Fears and anxieties are like monsters in our lives, suggests Matthew McKay in *Your Life on Purpose*, which is based on theories of acceptance and commitment therapy. And those monster fears and anxieties are loud, disruptive, and can often prevent us from heading in the direction we want to go. He offers a variation on the following exercise:

Picture yourself driving a bus down the road, when all of a sudden, a group of monsters jump into the road, yelling at you, waving their arms and baring their scraggly teeth. You slam on the brakes. All of a sudden, these monsters are all over you. Some are climbing up the front of the bus, others are just lying in the road in protest so you don't hit the accelerator again. You're stuck—and surrounded by your fear and anxiety monsters.

Here's the tough realization: you're not going to escape your monsters. These same ones or others may be with you for the rest of your life. If you can't push them out of the way and you can't outrun them, there's only one way to move your bus forward toward your purpose. "Just open the door and accept them as part of your life," writes Matthew McKay.

> Eventually, they'll take their seats in the back. They'll still jump up and wave their arms from time to time. They'll yell their threats and epithets and try to scare and discourage you. You can see them in the mirror and you can hear their cacophony. And sometimes they'll probably try to tell you where and how to drive the bus. They may even try to grab the wheel. But here's what's changed: [Your fears and anxieties] aren't in front of you anymore, keeping you stuck. You can put the bus in gear and head straight for what you value. You're taking them with you, along with all their upset, and you can still move. You are the driver and ultimately you are in charge of where the bus will go.

EXERCISE 10.6

Facing the Monsters and Anxieties

Write down your five biggest monsters and anxieties.

_____

_____

_____

_____

_____

Look over your list of fears and anxieties. Which ones are the biggest monsters in your way as you drive your bus toward a purpose and your desired future?

This step is a big one—and you might not be ready to do it quite yet. But it's a good goal to have. Not only do you need to identify your fears and anxieties, but you've got to invite them along for the ride so that you can move forward toward your purpose.

Self-Doubt

The fears and anxieties that you've listed in these exercises all add up to feelings of inadequacy—feelings that you aren't enough of what it takes to succeed or live your purpose. But remember the message from *The Wizard of Oz*? The Tin Man, Scarecrow, and Lion traveled all over Oz trying to find the Wizard who would make them whole—who would give them—respectively—a heart, a brain, and the courage to succeed. Of course, when they found the Wizard, they each discovered they were already enough; they had inside of themselves the things they were seeking all along.

Sometimes you feel like you aren't enough because you are comparing yourself to others. Other times you are focusing on your fears and anxieties—the negative feelings—rather than your positive feelings and your successful actions.

Combating self-doubt requires focusing on your strengths and being grateful for your many wins. One way to do this—a favorite in my family—is to celebrate incremental successes and little victories with gratitude. There's no need to wait to celebrate when the thesis is finished; you can celebrate completing a chapter or a detailed outline. Life doesn't have to be perfect for you to be grateful. These kinds of mini-celebrations help you focus on what you can accomplish and keep you away from wallowing in fear and anxiety.

Being grateful means acknowledging the gifts you've been given and using them in a meaningful—purposeful—way. No matter how dire things seem, if you think about it, you can find someone or something for which you are grateful every step of the way.

Inaction breeds fear and doubt. Action breeds confidence and courage. If you want to conquer fear, do not sit home and think about it. Go out and get busy.

—DALE CARNEGIE, AUTHOR

As a starting point, try being grateful for all your gifts and the good experiences that have brought you where you are now. You might consider writing a letter to a mentor, family member, or some other important person in your life whom you've never properly thanked for helping you get where you are today. Or you could write a letter to God, the Universe, or Mother Nature, saying, "Thank you for my own particular group of talents, strengths, and skills."

Gratitude can positively impact your psychological well-being and is correlated with feelings of purpose in your life. Put another way, the more grateful you are for the blessings you have in life, the more likely you are to overcome your fears and anxieties so that you can find and follow your path of purpose.

EXERCISE 10.7

Overcoming the "I'm Not Enough" Mantra

1. Acknowledge your daily accomplishments. Little things count, like getting out of bed when your alarm goes off or getting to all of your classes on time. Did you let someone pull ahead of you in traffic? Did you resist eating something unhealthy or spending unnecessarily? None of these are huge, but all are little things that count. Write out at least five things you've done today that are on track to living your statement of purpose.

_____

_____

_____

_____

2. Write a thank-you note to God, the Universe, or Mother Nature for making you you. Think about the talents, strengths, and skills you are most grateful for, and tell the recipient of your letter how you are thinking about using them.

_____

_____

_____

_____

_____

_____

3. Write a letter of gratitude to a mentor, family member, or person in your life you've never properly thanked for helping you get where you are today. Tell him or her where you hope to go, too.

_____

_____

_____

_____

_____

_____

4. Keep a gratitude journal. For five days, write about "topics that will create a happier future," suggests Richard Wiseman in _59 Seconds_. On day one, write about things for which you are grateful. On day two, write about some wonderful experiences in your life—times when you felt loved or content—and describe specifically how you felt at the time. On day three, write about what the future

might look like if you achieved your goals. For day four, write about someone important to you and why you care about them. On day five, review the previous week and write about three things that went really well for you.

Day 1:

_____

_____

_____

Day 2:

_____

_____

_____

Day 3:

_____

_____

_____

Day 4:

_____

_____

_____

Day 5:

_____

_____

_____

A Sample Gratitude Journal

Monday: I am grateful for my loving family, my great friends, and my fraternity brothers.

Tuesday: One of the greatest experiences I had in my life was my brother's wedding. It was great to see two families come together as one.

Wednesday: If I'm able to achieve my life goals, the future will look a lot like my brother's: I will be living a comfortable life doing what I love and being able to enjoy awesome experiences.

Thursday: One of the most important people in my life is my mother. She brought me into this world and showed me unconditional love and support.

Friday: This week I was able to successfully excel in two exams and possibly a third. We'll see in thirty minutes! Also, I gave an awesome presentation to my research director.

—Martin

▣ PLOT TWIST 3: THE PEANUT GALLERY

Friends

Friends can be a strong support system as you identify what's meaningful and make commitments to living purposefully, or they can be frenemies to your dreams by dissuading you from seeing the bigger picture. Think of these scenarios:

- ▸ Your friends are supportive of your purpose in theory, but they nag or tease you when you need to work or prioritize your future goals over going to a party or hanging out here and now.

- ▸ Your best friend initially seems supportive of your goals but then starts cautioning you with warnings that you might not be "enough"—not old enough, organized enough, serious enough—to pursue your goals. Is she jealous? Is he worried that your other interests might detract from time to hang out?

- ▸ In your social group, trying isn't considered cool. The go-with-the-flow attitude prevails, and you're worried that by admitting to your friends that you care about something, you'll be ridiculed.

EXERCISE 10.8

Friendly Fire

Think and write about your experiences with friends. Have you ever experienced any of these discouraging situations? Or have your friends been supportive of your goals and steps toward a purposeful life?

_____

_____

_____

Parents

Mark, a senior in college, was majoring in business. His father was a businessman and Mark knew that it was expected that he'd go into the same field. But he hated his economics and business classes. He loved, however, his architecture and art classes. Over winter break, he raised his concerns with his father, who immediately became frustrated and angry.

"You're a senior," Mark's father exploded. "I've paid for four years of college, and now when you're months away from graduation, you're telling me that you've changed your mind and don't want to get a degree in business? What, are you going to be an artist? Not with my money."

Hurt and even more confused, Mark found guidance in the father of one of his close friends—a coffee-shop owner who took Mark under his wing and taught him a process for discovering what career path he should take. This is the plot of *Finding Your Way: Discovering the Truth about You*, a fable that authors Dan Webster and Randy Gravitt published in hopes of helping young adults overcome parental pressure and live their individual life purposes.

Mark "knew there had to be more to his future than just getting a job and making a lot of money," Webster and Gravitt write. "His dad had gone that route and it had turned him into a jerk. Mark refused to go down the same path. Looking at all the different stars, Mark knew people were just as different. 'I will find my way,' he said out loud as he headed back to his room."

Our parents are our primary socializers. They gave us life and—ideally—support us as we figure out our individual journeys. But some of the best-intentioned parents see our future through the lens of the personal choices they have made, and pressure us to live out their dreams rather than ours. Not all parents do this, of course—and you may have great parents who see you exactly for who you are. But if you related to Mark's story, take some time to answer these questions.

Exercise 10.9

Parental Pressure

What are your parents' expectations? Do you feel pressure to achieve as much or more than your parents? In what ways, specifically? Do you feel pressured to make a certain amount of money, have a certain type of degree, or live in a certain type of home? Are these pressures explicit—that is, have your parents talked to you about their hopes?—or implicit, meaning that you infer them from somewhere? While you may have addressed some of these issues in Exercise 10.1, this exercise is meant to help you explore your relationship with your parents. Consider these questions in the space below.

1. I have spoken with my parents about my ideas about living my life purpose, and this was their reaction:

_____

_____

_____

2. If my parents could design my future for me, it would look like this:

_____

_____

_____

3. Thinking specifically about *money*, *status*, and *prestige*, I feel that my parents expect me to have, be, or do the following:

_____

_____

_____

4. Thinking specifically about *education* and *career*, I feel that my parents expect me to have, be, or do the following:

_____

_____

_____

5. You can love and admire your parents, while also being different from them. How are your vision, purpose, and goals similar to and different from the beliefs of your parents?

_____

_____

_____

▦ PLOT TWIST 4: CHOICES, CHOICES EVERYWHERE

Every day you're faced with the choice of what to do with your time. And every day you make a choice to use your time in a way that's in keeping with your values and purpose, or to take another path.

Think of it this way: Each day you've got 57,600 seconds (after a good night's sleep). If I gave you 57,600 dollars to spend, you'd spend it all, right? Every last cent, I bet. But if you think about what you did yesterday, I'd wager that much of your time wasn't spent living in a way that's in keeping with your values and purpose.

This is where choice comes in: How are you using your time?

"When our activities don't support our deepest values we feel lost, adrift and rudderless—sometimes even frantic," writes psychologist Matthew McKay, who introduces this metaphor in *Your Life on Purpose*. We make ourselves frantic in three big ways:

▸ Making "nonchoice" choices when values collide

▸ Procrastination

▸ Busyness without purpose

In this last section I offer three exercises to help you consider how procrastination, busyness, and colliding values affect your ability to live a purposeful life.

Colliding Values

As we saw in chapter 5, values can compete for your time, energy, and resources. Work can keep you from family and friends. Time devoted to your family might keep you from making new friends. Time devoted to commitments to others keeps you from time for yourself and your own interests.

We all wear a lot of hats, and our different responsibilities and goals can often conflict. You might have to work a few part-time jobs while in school so that you won't be saddled with too much debt after graduation. Maybe you faced a choice about missing your best friend's birthday party or passing an exam in a class where you were struggling. Perhaps you were absent from an important lecture because you had to be at an away game for your sports team.

There's no right answer about what to do in any of these scenarios, but the goal is to find some balance so that you're not always ignoring one value in favor of another.

You cannot be wimpy out there on the dream-seeking trail.
Dare to break through barriers, to find your own path.
—LES BROWN, MOTIVATIONAL SPEAKER

EXERCISE 10.10

When Values Collide

Think about a time in which you were faced with a clash of values. What were the circumstances, and what did you decide?

_____

_____

_____

_____

_____

_____

In this situation, did you

▶ Go for the "I can have it all, but not at the same time" attitude and follow one value more than another for a while?

▶ Decide that "it's all about balance" and try to switch back and forth between values so they each got some time?

▶ Follow some other path?

Which path did you choose? And how did things turn out?

_____

_____

_____

_____

_____

> "*I*t is always surprising how small a part of life is taken up by meaningful moments. Most often they're over before they start, even though they cast a light on the future and make the person who originated them unforgettable."
> —ANNA AND THE KING (1999)

When values collide, it's all about prioritizing. Sometimes you can combine interests—you can take your friends along on a service trip, or you can find a part-time job that has some downtime so that you can do homework at your desk—but other times you need to make a choice between diverging opportunities.

The path of least resistance—just going with the flow and seeing what happens—is itself a choice, but not usually one based on a thoughtful consideration of your values, and it usually won't lead you toward a purposeful life.

Procrastination

Procrastination—the decision to put off until tomorrow what should be done today—is something we all do. My bet is that you're procrastinating when it comes to living a purposeful life.

- ▶ "I'll think about vision and purpose later, after I get out of school and figure out my life."
- ▶ "I'll think of my vision for social change in my community later, when I've got more money and can really make a difference."
- ▶ "As long as I brainstorm now, I can wait to put the ideas into action later—at least until the summer, when things aren't as hectic with school."

Sound familiar? When it comes to pursuing a purposeful life, we often delay, delay, delay. Sometimes we've got ideas and the desire to do great things, but it's when too much is going that we get distracted.

Delay is the most effective form of denial. Procrastination can be dangerous when you put off values and parts of yourself for an undetermined time. If you leave it for too far in the future, it's as if it'll never happen.

> ▶ "Even though I don't have to financially, I could just get a job at Starbucks for a few years and then apply to grad school . . . later."
> ▶ "I want a family, but I don't have to think about that until I'm, like, thirty-five or forty."

Other times, procrastination can come from that fatalistic feeling that it's all meaningless, so why expend the effort? Stacey, a student in one of my classes a few years ago, said, "I find it impossible to plan for the future and find myself thinking about the very moment or second I am in. Because nothing else truly exists. Time is a made-up concept, and the future is too ambiguous."

Stacey's statement was spoken like a true philosopher—and a chronic procrastinator. The future isn't predictable, and in that sense, procrastination isn't totally illogical. Delaying work on a project might enable you to get more information about how to do it well. The project might become unnecessary. The world could end, or you could get hit by a bus.

But this fatalistic attitude doesn't typically lead to a particularly happy or successful outlook on life, psychologists find. I challenged Stacey to think about why she had this fatalistic attitude: Afraid of failure? Grumpy because other people seem to be bossing her around? Bored with her current job? Most likely, Stacey just needed to rethink her purpose.

Look back at your vision, purpose, and purpose-based commitments to change. You're probably not powering through this book all at once, so it's been a few weeks since you made those commitments. Have you put them into action? If not, why not? Spend some time thinking and writing about how and why you're procrastinating—and what you can do to get focused.

In his bestselling book *The 7 Habits of Highly Effective People*, Stephen Covey discusses the battle between the important things (taking steps to live purpose-fully) and the urgent things (our immediate demands, such as exams and work responsibilities) in our lives. Balancing the important and the urgent is always a challenge.

EXERCISE 10.11

Procrastination

When it comes to living a purposeful life and working toward your vision for change, are you procrastinating? If so, why—and how?

_____

_____

_____

_____

_____

What are three goals or rewards you could offer yourself to keep you on track to accomplish some of your goals and help you live a purposeful life with less procrastinating?

1. _____

_____

_____

2. _____

_____

_____

3. _____

_____

_____

The life you have led doesn't need to be the only life you have.

—ANNA QUINDLEN, JOURNALIST

▨ BUSY DOES NOT ALWAYS MEAN PURPOSEFUL

Even though I'm inundating you with lists and exercises, Barbara Braham, in her workbook *Finding Your Purpose: A Guide to Personal Fulfillment*, cautions you that busy does not mean successful or purposeful. Life may be so busy that it drowns out the inner voice that will tell you your purpose. Goals without a purpose are fairly meaningless, and your job is to turn down the volume of life and listen so that you can find the right path to direct your energies.

Just by working through these chapters, you've taken time out to be thoughtful and listen to your inner voice. Psychologists recommend that all of us incorporate a little bit of silence and meditation (broadly defined) into our lives. Quiet time is something you can make work for you whatever your personality.

EXERCISE 10.12

Relax Your Mind

Try one of these tips below to calm your busy mind. Write down what you experienced, both positive and negative. Does calming your mind give you energy or new ideas about living your vision and purpose?

1. Go for a walk. Take a stroll outside for twenty or thirty minutes. Leave your phone and all other devices behind, so that it's just you and nature (or the city)

for a few minutes. Notice what's going on around you: New neighbors moving in? Is it breezy? Are you anxious without your gadgets? Pay attention to all your senses and feelings.

2. Take a time-out. Again, turn off your gadgets and do something for yourself. Take a hot bath, read a book, do a craft project, bake something, or swing on the swings. Be with yourself and see what happens.

3. Write in your journal. Type or handwrite your thoughts—deep and banal—about what's going on in your life, how it makes you feel, and what you'd like to change. Journaling is an effective method for brainstorming about how you are living your vision for change, the challenges of living a life of purpose, and your hopes for the future. No one else needs to read your journal, so forget about grammar and spelling and just dump out your feelings.

4. Make a list. One of my favorite calming techniques is to make a list of every-thing that is bothering me, everything I have to do, or everyone I need to call, email, follow up with, or thank. This kind of big data download frees up your mind because you don't have to hold all the worries in your head; they are on a piece of paper, a to-do list on your computer, or sticky notes on your desk. Then you can have the satisfaction of crossing things off as you accomplish your tasks.

I tried calming technique   1   2   3   4

Describe what you did, whether you thought this exercise was useful, whether it helped you refocus or gave you new ideas about your vision and purpose, and so on.

_____

_____

_____

▪ SORTING THINGS OUT

My hope is that this chapter has helped you confront some of the big obstacles that might get in your way as you try to live a purposeful life. You've done excellent work in this chapter, facing your fears and anxieties and making plans to overcome the obstacles that might get in the way of living with a purpose mindset. If your head is reeling, you're not alone—but I can also tell you that this chapter had the biggest impact on my *Big Picture* testers.

> *Vulnerability is the birthplace of innovation, creativity, and change.*
> —BRENÉ BROWN, AUTHOR AND RESEARCHER

EXERCISE 10.13

Untwisting the Plot Twists

Look back through the plot-twist exercises you've just completed. What are the five biggest obstacles in your path—either that came up in the worksheet or that you have thought of on your own? How will you work to overcome them?

Obstacle 1 and How to Overcome It

Obstacle 2 and How to Overcome It

_____

_____

Obstacle 3 and How to Overcome It

_____

_____

Obstacle 4 and How to Overcome It

_____

_____

Obstacle 5 and How to Overcome It

_____

_____

Are you feeling relieved, calm, and productive? If not, the next chapter is where you reach out to your cast of supporting characters to ask for help. Talking through the work you've done so far—and getting their advice for next steps or new ways of thinking—will help you reach even more clarity in your purpose journey.

CHAPTER 11

Your Supporting Cast

Earlier in the book we met Kristie, a dancer whose heart condition prevented her from following her first passion. After searching for her purpose, Kristie began teaching yoga and reunited with her body. "All my knowledge of anatomy from years of dancing and studying movement in dance came back to me. It was like picking up an old hat: it fit perfectly," she said.

But as with most life stories, things don't wrap up neatly with a bow. One day, doing Child's Pose at a yoga class, her defibrillator went off and shocked her. "I spent the weekend trying to process this. Yoga taught me to be vulnerable and open and in the moment. I sat with it and invited the feelings in for tea, as a teacher had once said to me."

At the hospital on Monday, Kristie was told her pacemaker had broken and that surgery was required that afternoon. She was alone since it was the last minute. During the surgery—for which the patient is mostly awake—Kristie had an overwhelming feeling of being violated.

"When I didn't know what else to do, I fell back on my training and I meditated. I used my basic mantra: *so hum*, I am that, that I am. It's a Sanskrit mantra that is really the sound of your breath. I meditated on the idea that I am the energy, not the body in surgery. I stopped feeling scared and violated. I am not my body. I am before and beyond this. My inner guru took over. I felt a deep connection to the 'I' or to the spirit."

But after a week of recovery, Kristie was depressed again. She couldn't pick up her children, and her husband was stressed from doing it all. "I was so tired. I didn't want to deal with it. I flushed my painkillers down the toilet because I was scared I'd take them all at once."

Kristie reached out to her teachers and mentors for help. One of Kristie's original yoga instructors listened patiently to her story and said, "I see a really wise, empathetic teacher being born. And we all know how painful it is to be born." This was language that Kristie could understand. "So I went back into therapy. I meditated. And while I'm still not allowed to do several poses for medical reasons, I slowly got back into yoga.

"I stopped thinking about how things should be and started seeing things how they are. I said I wanted to work with heart patients and to help them through yoga. Three days later, a job opened at a prestigious health center and I got an interview."

Today Kristie is a stress management expert and teaches prenatal yoga. She is also teaching dancers to do yoga and is working for the American Heart Association teaching yoga as well.

"I'm very confident in my path. There's so much I want to do. I'm working incredibly hard and teaching fourteen classes this week, but I don't stress about it because it's my path. I have a deep faith as a result of finding my purpose.

"Be open to everything, but when you find your purpose, make sure your energy goes there. Be thoughtful about choices you make. It's okay to say no. And it's okay to begin again. Even if you stray from your purpose—just like breathing, you can begin again. As long as you are breathing, you can begin again.

"It was a slow awakening. I couldn't have done it alone. Your teachers and mentors enter when you are ready to learn," she said. Now Kristie tries to mentor others, including her students. "I turn my dancers away from the mirror. I love to remind them how good it feels to be in your body."

Kristie has surrounded herself with mentors and teachers who are at the top of their field. "Yes, I could be jealous of their success, but instead I ask them to mentor me. I learn from their example. Surround yourself with people who are good at what they do. Learn from their mistakes. Be humble enough to listen."

She has a tattoo of a lotus on her wrist with the mantra *so hum*. She got the tattoo a year to the day after her surgery. "The lotus starts in murky water because it can rise up and see the sun and blossom, and that's me."

✳ ✳ ✳

The movie of Kristie's life would be full of action and dramatic moments, realizations and commitments to living in a purposeful way. But we would see Kristie, the star of this purpose-based movie, surrounded by a supporting cast of characters—her family, her friends, and the valuable mentors and teachers who have guided and encouraged her.

Who influences you in your personal movie? Whom do you admire? Who are the costars in your documentary of meaning and purpose? Who are the supporting actors and actresses that make life possible?

▊ UNDER THE INFLUENCE

Certain authors influence the way we think, some special teachers open our eyes to possibilities, and effective leaders guide us in pursuit of a cause. No matter how self-reliant we are, we've received inspiration, help, and wisdom from others along the way.

Take a few minutes to think about the people who inspire you—their personal attributes, their vision, and what you learned about yourself from them. None of these people are perfect, of course, and your job isn't going to be copying their lives. Instead, identifying who inspires and influences you can give you clues to your unique purpose.

You've had many teachers in your life. Your parents and caregivers were your first teachers. They modeled basic behaviors and (hopefully) taught you things like how to share, brush your teeth, and tie your shoes. Your siblings may be influential people in your life, and you might even be inspired by their lives. But push yourself a little further: Who else has inspired and influenced you? To help you brainstorm, think about:

Artists	Friends	Motivational speakers
Athletes	Historical figures	Politicians
Authors	Inventors	Schoolteachers and professors
Extended family	The less fortunate	Social activists

Teachers can teach by explaining or conveying information, but they can also teach and inspire by example—how they lived their lives, how they reacted to challenges, how they demonstrated patience.

Sometimes things that teachers say stick in your head—forever. It might be something your best friend's mom said to you when you were thirteen, the way your French teacher carried herself, or the unfailing smile your Sunday school teacher had each week. It could be a speech, a painting, a song, or the ideas of an inventor.

EXERCISE 11.1

Influential People

Who inspires you? Who are your teachers? Spend some time thinking about these influential people in your life—and what they taught you.

I am inspired and influenced by

Name: _____

This person's vision or purpose is/was _____

_____

_____

This person taught me _____

_____

_____

Name: _____

This person's vision or purpose is/was _____

_____

_____

This person taught me _____

_____

_____

Name: _____

This person's vision or purpose is/was _____

_____

_____

This person taught me _____

_____

_____

▉ MENTORS

No man is an island—and you're not, either. While a lot of deep thinking is best done alone, trusted mentors can offer the reality check that's needed to turn vision into purpose and help you achieve your short-term and long-term goals. These are the costars or supporting cast of characters who will offer pivotal words of wisdom to propel your movie forward.

You might find a mentor at work, like Fred did. Fred left his job at an advertising agency to live his purpose by founding an executive recruitment firm, and he says it was the support of his mentor—who was his longtime boss—that helped him make the leap. "My mentor put me in a position to learn and grow by giving me assignments that would stretch me and give me greater visibility to senior management. He and I clicked on a personal level and we enjoyed each other's company, so work seemed like more fun that it might otherwise have been. Naturally, I didn't always succeed in everything I tried, but I always felt he was taking a real interest in my career, rather than just being my boss or manager."

Or your mentor might already be a major player in your personal life. Greg, who feels his purpose is to serve God in the ministry, said that a bishop at his church has been his most influential mentor. "After serving at the altar with my bishop for the first time at age eight, he asked me to put away his large, silver staff. Being a young child, I didn't ever expect for him to ask me to do this, but was even more taken aback when he spoke to me, asking about my interests and my life as I carefully put away his liturgical staff, piece by piece, for travel. When I had finished and wrapped it up, handing it back to him, he told me that I would 'make a great priest one day.'" After that initial conversation, the bishop continued to advise and guide Greg, and he says, "Those words have always stuck with me, and even today I intend to serve the church as a member of the clergy."

For Sam, who is now active in suicide prevention after a student in his dorm committed suicide when he was in college, it was a board member at a breakfast fundraiser. "She leaned over and said, 'You should join us. We need a man on the board, and even better that you're a college student.' Within two months, I'd become a board member. She handed me a lesson: When you see potential, encourage it. I'm forever thankful for her guidance."

To identify mentors, think about people who know you well, and whom you trust. You don't need a ton of people. In fact, just one good mentor will do.

How to Find a Mentor

1. Make a list of people whom you know well and trust.

2. Of those people, whom do you admire most? Take some time to think about why you admire them. If they are on your inspirational or teachers' list, all the better. Make some notes on what about them makes them good mentors for you.

3. Cast a wide net. Mentors aren't necessarily a professional thing. Indeed, a mentor who can guide you and serve as a sounding board on personal issues is ideal. And mentors don't have to be older than you are.

4. Play it cool. Don't ask someone out of the blue, "Will you be my mentor?" as that would be a little creepy. Instead, ask for some specific advice, and use this workbook as a jumping-off point. For example, "I'm reading this great book on finding purpose, and I've made a lot of headway on my own. Can we meet for coffee next week so I that can run some of my ideas by you and ask you a few questions about your journey?"

5. Make it fun. Mentoring sessions can happen over coffee or lunch, or at the nail salon . . . wherever you can talk about big issues without too many interruptions.

6. Show your gratitude. If the relationship can be reciprocal—and no matter how much of a big dog your mentor is, you can always do something small for someone—then it'll be a better and longer-lasting relationship.

It's all part of paying it forward. You're going to get help now in these early years, and then someday you'll be the mentor. People want to help. Someone helped them, and you'll hopefully help someone else in the future, too.

If you are looking for an older mentor, tap your school's alumni connections: Folks who share the same alma mater might be more willing to help you out. If you're looking for a general life mentor, consider someone in your faith community or in a professional or social group that matches with your interests.

EXERCISE 11.2

My List of Possible Mentors

Once you've figured out whom you want to confide in, take notes in advance and write out some specific questions before planning your in-person meeting. Having the meeting in person is especially important.

Texting or email might be your go-to medium for most communication, but face-to-face connections have benefits. In her book, *The Village Effect*, psychologist Susan Pinker argues that in-person encounters help build more engaging and meaningful connections with our families, friends, colleagues, and communities. By cultivating and experiencing a face-to-face connection with others, we help build learning, happiness, resilience, and longevity, as well as develop a deeper potential for friendship and longer-lasting connections.

EXERCISE 11.3

Interview Potential Mentors

Make a coffee or lunch date with a potential mentor and consider asking some versions of the following questions:

Questions about Them

▶ If you could be remembered for one thing, what would it be?

▶ If you could change one thing about the world, what would it be?

▶ Who are you without your family, job, or money?

▶ How would you describe your personal purpose?

Questions about You

▸ What do you see as my most important strengths?

▸ What do you see as my areas for growth?

▸ In which roles could I thrive, and why?

▸ What kinds of roles and situations should I avoid, and why?

▸ What is my greatest potential?

▸ I've written vision and purpose statements [read them or share them in advance via email]. Any advice on how I can clarify and live these?

The most important thing of all about mentors is to *listen to them*.

Too often we are wrapped up in our questions, in proving ourselves, and in talking about ourselves that we forget to listen. You won't learn much from listening to yourself talk, so make sure to listen to your mentor's answers. Take notes. Ask follow-ups. The goal isn't to get answers for the interview; the goal is to learn from your mentor's experiences and wisdom, and to consider their suggestions.

You won't always agree with what your mentor tells you. Also, "listen to them" is not the same as "follow exactly what they say." But since you've put some thought into why this person might be a good guide for you, it's worth considering their advice, and perhaps even testing it out.

For example, as she completed this chapter, Sara identified a classmate, Julie, as a potential peer mentor.

> Julie actually asked me to hang out first. While we were driving around, she pointed out landmarks in the city and showed me around. She showed me her apartment and gave me great advice on renting next year. I learned a lot from her just enjoying our Friday night out. Over dinner we discussed everything from our future plans, to guys, to deeper issues regarding faith. I found that Julie and I share the same values, and she is definitely a strong woman who is going places in life. In my mind, she would be a great example to follow.

Sara asked Julie questions about her decision to transfer schools, what keeps her faith so strong, and what made her decide to go into medicine. Sara also received Julie's feedback and advice on what kinds of internships and part-time jobs might be best for her, what skills she might focus on in the future, and what Bible verses might spark meaningful reflection.

For of all sad words of tongue or pen,
The saddest are these: "It might have been."
—JOHN GREENLEAF WHITTIER, POET

After spending time with Julie, Sara took the following notes:

I am definitely going to look into the Centers for Disease Control and what they are doing in aging. I am also going to follow a bit of advice she gave me about getting great internships and jobs: Julie said that if you really want a job, just apply for it; simple as that. She advised me not to worry too much about my age or qualifications because if I am not qualified the worst that could happen is that I end up where I started.

Mentor 1 Worksheet

Name: _____

Reasons I choose this person as a mentor:

_____

_____

Questions I want to ask them about themselves, their challenges, and their experiences:

_____

_____

_____

Questions I want to ask them about me, my ideas about purpose, and my goals going forward:

_____

_____

_____

Notes from our conversation, and things I'm going to think about or do:

_____

_____

_____

MENTOR 2 WORKSHEET

Name: _____

Reasons I choose this person as a mentor:

_____

_____

Questions I want to ask them about themselves, their challenges, and their experiences:

_____

_____

_____

_____

Questions I want to ask them about me, my ideas about purpose, and my goals going forward:

_____

_____

_____

_____

Notes from our conversation, and things I'm going to think about or do:

_____

_____

_____

_____

Your Costars

Depending on whom you've chosen as a mentor, it's possible that you will have a fairly formal relationship. Sometimes a mentor is a boss, pastor, or professor—not exactly someone you're having drinks with on a regular basis. So in addition to your inspirational and influential mentor (or mentors), you should create your own supporting cast.

Your supporting cast is a group of people whom you trust to advise you when making big life decisions. You turn to these people when you need a reality check and when you are deciding among options that will dictate an important life transition.

These are the main costars of your movie, and you likely already have some of these people in your life: Your best friends, your parents and siblings, and perhaps an older adult in whom you confide and ask for advice along the way. But on your journey to identify and live your purpose, you'll need advice from a variety of different voices—not just your inner circle—and that's where a well-chosen supporting cast really helps.

Our best friends are not typically the ones who help us get a job or see the world in a new way. It's the folks whom we see less frequently, with whom we're *less* close that challenge us to think differently and head in new directions. If we only hang out with folks who are similar to us, we'll be limited in the way we think.

EXERCISE 11.4

Your Supporting Cast

Think about those eight big areas of your life again:

Family	Education	Work	Physical
Financial	Spiritual	Relationships	Free time

For each area, think of two people you might ask for advice and guidance. These should be people from whom you would seek trusted support on your path to purpose. One of the people you list should be someone very close to you—in the inner circle—and someone whom you might talk to often. But use this exercise also to identify the people you're not so close to, but who can still help you achieve your vision and live your purpose. For each category, think of someone in your outer circle, too, whom you'd periodically ask for advice on the big stuff, and whose opinion you'd trust in that particular area.

If some of the life areas don't apply to you right now, just disregard them and substitute another aspect of your life that seems more relevant. And if you can only come up with one person for some areas, that's okay, too. The idea is to brainstorm on how you can branch out to and get support from a variety of different people.

Family

Inner circle cast member:

_____

Outer circle cast member:

_____

Education

Inner circle cast member:

_____

Outer circle cast member:

_____

Work

Inner circle cast member:

_____

Outer circle cast member:

_____

Physical

Inner circle cast member:

_____

Outer circle cast member:

_____

Financial

Inner circle cast member:

_____

Outer circle cast member:

_____

Spiritual

Inner circle cast member:

_____

Outer circle cast member:

_____

Relationships

Inner circle cast member:

_____

Outer circle cast member:

_____

Free Time

Inner circle cast member:

_____

Outer circle cast member:

_____

The point of mentors and a supporting cast member is to create a sounding board to help you crystallize your vision, live your individual purpose, and achieve your goals. The following exercise guides you through the process of soliciting your mentors' input.

EXERCISE 11.5

Get Feedback on Your Vision, Purpose, and Goals

Pick one person in your inner circle and one person in your outer circle. Email or read them your vision statement, your purpose statement, your purpose-based commitments, and the goals you've set toward them. Then ask them for feedback.

▶ Do they have any advice on how you can achieve these goals?

▶ Any suggestions for next steps?

▶ Might they know any people or organizations that could help you?

▶ Any words of wisdom or encouragement they can offer?

This is the inner circle advice I've received from _____ ,

who is [describe who this person is in relation to you] _____ :

_____

_____

_____

Based on this advice, I am going to consider doing, changing, or thinking about the following things:

_____

_____

_____

This is the outer circle advice I've received from _____ ,

who is [describe who this person is in relation to you] _____ :

_____

_____

_____

Based on this advice, I am going to consider doing, changing, or thinking about the following things:

_____

_____

_____

Speaking with your mentors isn't a onetime process and shouldn't be rushed. Also, some of your answers and ideas earlier in the book may change after your mentoring meetings. You might have new ideas that you want to incorporate into your movie reel, or you may even need to take a few weeks for reflection on your next steps.

Please reach out to others in this purpose journey. There's no reason to go it alone, and you don't get extra points for self-sufficiency.

CHAPTER 12

Postproduction

> When you see what you're here for, the world begins to mirror
> your purpose in a magical way. It's almost as if you suddenly find
> yourself on a stage in a play that was written expressly for you.
> —Betty Sue Flowers

Throughout this book I've asked you to consider how you personally can create meaning for yourself and others on a small scale now—and perhaps on a larger scale in the future.

Running through these chapters was the metaphor of producing and directing the movie of your life: What do you want to show your kids and grandkids about how you've used your talents and time here on Earth in a meaningful way? How do you want to take action to address problems, create solutions, and touch the lives of others so that you will inspire future generations to a life of outward-focused purpose, too?

Let's wrap it up by taking it all into postproduction—putting the final touches on your movie.

■ THE BIG PICTURE IN REVIEW

The Reel Image

Like any good movie, there has to be a star—and that's you, with all your gifts and strengths. But the plot of the movie is driven by your core values. How will those values affect your life and make this movie a reality?

You've done a lot of work putting together the different elements of your movie. If you haven't already, fill in all the parts of your movie reel and post it somewhere where it will inspire you to lights, camera, action . . . and meaning!

EXERCISE 12.1

Your Movie Reel

Perhaps you've been filling in a draft of the reel as you went through the book. If so, feel free to use one of the extra movie-reel images provided in Appendix B to create a clean, shareable copy. Perhaps you haven't added anything to your reel yet, and if that's the case, now's the time to write them down:

▶ Your skills, talents, and strengths are found in chapter 4 and go in the reel itself.

▶ Your core values are found in chapter 5 and go in the center of the spool.

▶ What you love to do is found in chapter 6 and goes in the reel itself.

▶ Your vision statement, found in chapter 7, can be placed on the lower left.

▶ Similarly, your purpose statement from chapter 8, or the phrase you crafted for the tombstone exercise at the end of that chapter, can be the guide to filling in the center bottom of the movie reel.

▶ On the far right, list the top purpose-based commitments for each area of your life from chapter 9.

Your Tagline

"After a night they can't remember comes a day they'll never forget." "Sometimes the only way to stay sane is to go a little crazy." These two movie taglines pack a big punch. Your interest is piqued and you want to know more: What's going to happen?

Perhaps your tagline will be a quote you love that guides you. Maybe it's something you say all the time. Coming up with a tagline or slogan for your life is a good way to crystallize your commitment to purposeful living, to a particular vision, and to being the change you hope to see in the world, as Gandhi said.

Sam said his tagline might be, "Live life in the now, so that I can tell stories in the future." Amy suggested that the simple statement, "Love God, Love People, Love Life," would best sum up her purpose, while Melanie debated between two statements: "Keep your head up so that you can see the doors that lead to better things," and "When surrounded by friends, it's easy to laugh at past mistakes and future fears." Actual movie taglines might give you some ideas, too.

Brainstorm on a snippet of text that might capture the movie of your life. Here are a few suggestions:

- ▶ Look carefully at your core values. What words jump out at you? How might you work with those keywords to generate ideas?
- ▶ Make your tagline unique to your purpose and vision for change. Don't make it too general.
- ▶ Keep it positive.

Movie Taglines to Spark Your Creativity

There's something about your first piece. —*American Pie* (1999)

Every man dies, not every man really lives. —*Braveheart* (1995)

Love is a force of nature. —*Brokeback Mountain* (2005)

They had a date with fate in Casablanca! —*Casablanca* (1942)

The true story of a real fake. —*Catch Me If You Can* (2002)

Sex. Clothes. Popularity. Is there a problem here? —*Clueless* (1995)

They took everything he had . . . except his rage.
—*Collateral Damage* (2002)

She brought a small town to its feet and a huge corporation
to its knees. —*Erin Brockovich* (2000)

There are 3.7 trillion fish in the ocean. They're looking for one.
—*Finding Nemo* (2003)

Don't get mad. Get everything. —*The First Wives Club* (1996)

What we do in life echoes in eternity. —*Gladiator* (2000)

Nothing is as simple as black and white. —*Pleasantville* (1998)

Does for rock and roll what *The Sound of Music*
did for hills. —*This Is Spinal Tap* (1984)

Bernie may be dead, but he's still the life of the party!
—*Weekend at Bernie's* (1989)

EXERCISE 12.2

Create Your Own Tagline

Write down your purpose-based life tagline. You can give two or three if you'd like. As you write out your tagline or taglines, you're looking for something that's catchy, but also something that speaks to you in a meaningful way.

_____

_____

_____

_____

Why did you choose this tagline? What does it mean to you, or what do you hope that it captures?

_____

_____

_____

 Once you are satisfied with your tagline, add it to your movie reel in Appendix B.

Your Theme Music

Theme music is usually played during the introduction, the title sequence, or the ending credits of a TV show, radio show, or movie. But for you as an individual, it's the song that plays in your head when important things happen, when you are pensive on a train watching the trees zip past, or at the cue-the-music moment when

Mine Your Playlist

Stumped about a theme song? Look at your music playlist, and list your ten most played songs. Then narrow it down to your top three favorites and listen to them carefully. Is there a lyric or line in the song that seems to guide you through your day? Is there a rhythm that gets you going or inspires you?

you finally decide to take the big step, make a change, and live your dreams.

Music elicits so many emotions; it can set the mood, bring back memories, or cue optimism or sadness. Ideally your theme song will help you embrace your purpose and give you the strength to continue to solider on in the face of challenges or just keep putting one foot in front of the other for another day.

Molly said her theme song was U2's "Beautiful Day," because not only did the music uplift her but the lyrics helped her keep life in perspective. Adam said David Gray's "Babylon" often popped into his head as he was moving toward a goal because he liked the image of acknowledging that, with patience, life's metaphorical traffic lights turn from red to green, encouraging you to live your purpose if you don't overthink things and are open to letting go a bit.

EXERCISE 12.3

Name That Tune

What's your theme song, or your top two or three?

_____

_____

_____

_____

Why did you choose this song? What does it mean to you, or what do you hope that it captures?

_____

_____

_____

_____

 Once you settle on a purpose-focused theme song, add it to your movie reel in Appendix B.

Your Sizzle Reel

In chapter 8, you fast-forwarded through thirty years of your life: identifying the core people in your family (and how you anticipate that changing over time), where you'll live and what it's like, what you do, what you worry about, what you hope for, and what you love. Look at the exercise on page 116 again. If you were screening a movie of your purpose-filled life to your grandkids and great-grandkids, what would be the highlights?

While this exercise is about creating a sizzle reel, let's make it a more *real* reel. As you consider your life's milestones, think about not only the accomplishment—the goal you are achieving—but the value behind the goal, how you feel, and what drives you to keep going. Also include some stumbling blocks and low moments that you had to overcome.

For example, Ellie values financial stability and excitement. Her vision is to educate all children regardless of their economic circumstances. When it came to purpose-based commitments, Ellie said her big one was to start a nonprofit to fund disadvantaged schools. Fast-forwarding fifty years into the future, Ellie said she would envision a movie trailer of her life with these highlights:

The smile on my face that first day I was able to set aside money from my paycheck to begin to fund a future charity. Hanging a sign outside the door of my new nonprofit, with my family proudly looking on. At least one or two clips to show that I fought through a lot, had my doubts about whether I could pull it off, and acknowledging my fears that I wasn't good enough. But follow that up with one of those montages where you see lots of short clips of me working with different schools, up late at night writing grants, taking my own kids to work with me so that they can see what I'm so passionate about, and then finally ending with a groundbreaking ceremony for a new building that a school for the disadvantaged has been able to build because of my nonprofit. Maybe a final clip where I hand over my nonprofit to someone else—to show that my vision will live on even after I retire or move on to focus on family or whatever else I want to do.

EXERCISE 12.4

Create a Trailer for Your Life Movie

What would your movie trailer look like? Visualizing the celebration of goals is easy, so don't place too much focus there. The values, purpose, and vision behind those goals make your movie significant, so think in those terms rather than just sharing a list of accomplishments.

Scene 1:

_____

_____

_____

_____

Scene 2:

_____

_____

_____

_____

Scene 3:

_____

_____

_____

_____

Scene 4:

_____

_____

_____

_____

Scene 5:

_____

_____

_____

_____

Are you inspired? Is that theme song running through your head?

■ DON'T STOP NOW

You've built up a lot of momentum as you worked through the exercises in this book. Maybe you feel like your path has been reaffirmed. Perhaps you are emboldened to switch majors or take new action. You may even still feel uncertain about next steps, and that's okay, too.

> "*Y*ou cannot live your life to please others. The choice must be yours." —ALICE IN WONDERLAND (2010)

Before you put this book away, I challenge you to do three things: Fill out your movie reel completely, share it with at least two people, and make it a priority to take one of those purpose-based commitments and turn it into action . . . *this week*.

Complete Your Movie Reel

If you've not been filling in the movie reel because you think it's just busywork, let me assure you that it's worth completing. Research shows that the most effective way to actually create change is to do something concrete and be proud of your efforts. Success in something relatively small, like completing a workbook, is a signal for success on larger things, like living out your purpose mindset. You've done a lot of work in this book, and now is the time to aggregate it into one place so that you can say, "Hey, I did that—and now I can conquer the world."

To finish what you've started here, go online to TheBigPicture.Life, where you can access a PDF version of the reel and other pieces of useful information.

Share Your Movie Reel

Public commitments to change are more likely to be successful than private commitments to change. Living out your purpose is no different. By telling people your vision, purpose, and goals, you're taking a stand—and you're more likely to make those purpose-based commitments a reality.

Consider sharing your movie reel first with a close friend, a significant other, or a parent. Get their feedback. Tell them about your experience with this book and what you're excited about in the future.

Then consider sharing your movie reel with a mentor, professor, or guidance counselor. Ask for their feedback on what you've compiled, as well as their recommendations on career, educational, and personal next steps that you might not have considered.

Lights, Camera . . . Action

Your purpose comes to life when you take action. Crank up the volume on your theme song and look back at the purpose-based commitments you made in Exercise 9.1. Now, pick one that you can take action on this week. It doesn't have to be a huge step—small steps toward change build our self-efficacy and boost our ability to take the next step—but turn that potential energy into kinetic energy right now with some purposeful action.

You can do it. It's your choice, and the time to start is now. That choice—embracing a purpose mindset and taking action toward what's most meaningful to you—is the most powerful one you'll ever make. As Dumbledore says in *Harry Potter and the Chamber of Secrets*, "It is not our abilities that show what we truly are . . . it is our choices."

Here's to purpose and possibilities.

Here's to your Big Picture.

IN 2012–13, I surveyed more than one thousand young adults and asked them questions about purpose and meaning. Below are selected answers. For more information, visit TheBigPicture.Life.

I feel good when I think of what I've done in the past and what I hope to do in the future.

☐	Absolutely untrue	0%
▧	Mostly/somewhat untrue	6%
▧	Neutral	17%
	Somewhat/mostly true	63%
▧	Absolutely true	14%

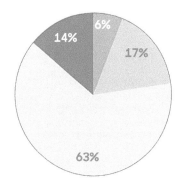

I live life one day at a time and don't really think about the future.

▧	Absolutely untrue	19%
	Mostly/somewhat untrue	56%
▧	Neutral	8%
▧	Somewhat/mostly true	16%
▧	Absolutely true	1%

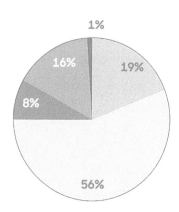

I used to set goals for myself, but now that seems like a waste of time.

▨ Absolutely untrue	35%
▨ Mostly/somewhat untrue	48%
▨ Neutral	8%
▨ Somewhat/mostly true	7%
▨ Absolutely true	2%

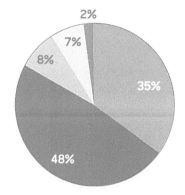

I enjoy making plans for the future and working to make them a reality.

▨ Absolutely untrue	1%
▨ Mostly/somewhat untrue	6%
▨ Neutral	8%
▨ Somewhat/mostly true	60%
▨ Absolutely true	25%

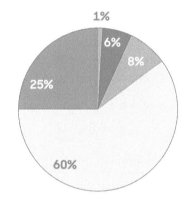

I am an active person in carrying out the plans I set for myself.

☐ Absolutely untrue	0%
▨ Mostly/somewhat untrue	7%
▨ Neutral	9%
▨ Somewhat/mostly true	68%
▨ Absolutely true	18%

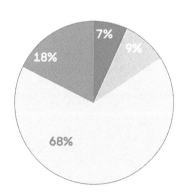

Some people wander aimlessly through life, but I am not one of them.

▨	Absolutely untrue	2%
▨	Mostly/somewhat untrue	14%
▨	Neutral	14%
	Somewhat/mostly true	48%
▨	Absolutely true	22%

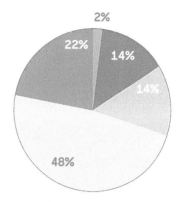

I find it satisfying to think about what I have accomplished in life.

▨	Absolutely untrue	1%
▨	Mostly/somewhat untrue	10%
▨	Neutral	12%
	Somewhat/mostly true	53%
▨	Absolutely true	24%

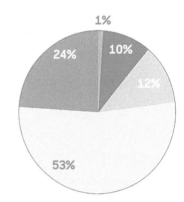

I understand my life's meaning.

▨	Absolutely untrue	11%
▨	Mostly/somewhat untrue	25%
▨	Neutral	33%
	Somewhat/mostly true	28%
▨	Absolutely true	3%

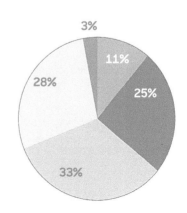

My life has a clear sense of purpose.

▨	Absolutely untrue	5%
▨	Mostly/somewhat untrue	19%
▨	Neutral	25%
▨	Somewhat/mostly true	45%
▨	Absolutely true	6%

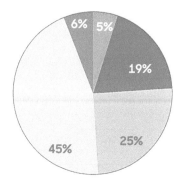

I have a good sense of what makes my life meaningful.

▨	Absolutely untrue	1%
▨	Mostly/somewhat untrue	10%
▨	Neutral	11%
▨	Somewhat/mostly true	63%
▨	Absolutely true	15%

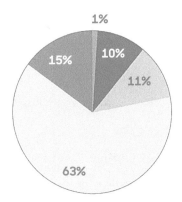

I have discovered a satisfying life purpose.

▨	Absolutely untrue	4%
▨	Mostly/somewhat untrue	20%
▨	Neutral	25%
▨	Somewhat/mostly true	42%
▨	Absolutely true	9%

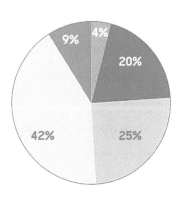

I am seeking a purpose or mission for my life.

▦	Absolutely untrue	2%
▦	Mostly/somewhat untrue	14%
▦	Neutral	16%
	Somewhat/mostly true	50%
▦	Absolutely true	18%

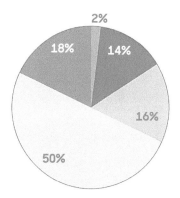

I am searching for meaning in my life.

▦	Absolutely untrue	3%
▦	Mostly/somewhat untrue	21%
▦	Neutral	18%
	Somewhat/mostly true	44%
▦	Absolutely true	14%

When I think about big life decisions (such as what major or career to pursue), I always think about how my purpose can guide my choice.

▦	Absolutely untrue	3%
▦	Mostly/somewhat untrue	15%
▦	Neutral	27%
	Somewhat/mostly true	44%
▦	Absolutely true	11%

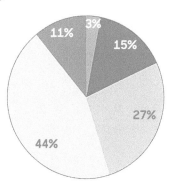

Religion or spirituality is important in my life.

▢	Absolutely untrue	20%
▢	Mostly/somewhat untrue	22%
▢	Neutral	13%
▢	Somewhat/mostly true	29%
▢	Absolutely true	16%

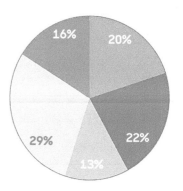

Appendix B: Blank Movie Reels

My Purpose in Each Role I Play:

Family: _____

Education: _____

Work: _____

Physical: _____

Financial: _____

Spiritual: _____

Relationships: _____

Free time: _____

Star Talents:

1. _____
2. _____
3. _____

Personal Strengths:

1. _____
2. _____
3. _____

Core Values:

1. _____
2. _____
3. _____

Useful Skills:

1. _____
2. _____
3. _____

What I Love to Do:

1. _____
2. _____
3. _____

As the star and producer of the movie of his/her life,
_____ is a person who
_____
_____
_____
_____

My Vision in Life Is to:

_____
_____
_____
_____

Tagline for the movie:

Theme song:

My Purpose in Each Role I Play:

Family: _____

Education: _____

Work: _____

Physical: _____

Financial: _____

Spiritual: _____

Relationships: _____

Free time: _____

Star Talents:
1. _____
2. _____
3. _____

Personal Strengths:
1. _____
2. _____
3. _____

Core Values:
1. _____
2. _____
3. _____

Useful Skills:
1. _____
2. _____
3. _____

What I Love to Do:
1. _____
2. _____
3. _____

As the star and producer of the movie of his/her life,
_____ is a person who
_____
_____
_____

My Vision in Life Is to:
_____
_____
_____
_____

Tagline for the movie:

Theme song:

My Purpose in Each Role I Play:

Family: _____

Education: _____

Work: _____

Physical: _____

Financial: _____

Spiritual: _____

Relationships: _____

Free time: _____

Star Talents:
1. _____
2. _____
3. _____

Personal Strengths:
1. _____
2. _____
3. _____

Core Values:
1. _____
2. _____
3. _____

Useful Skills:
1. _____
2. _____
3. _____

What I Love to Do:
1. _____
2. _____
3. _____

As the star and producer of the movie of his/her life,
_____ is a person who
_____

My Vision in Life Is to:
_____
_____
_____

Tagline for the movie:
_____

Theme song:

My Purpose in Each Role I Play:

Family: _____

Education: _____

Work: _____

Physical: _____

Financial: _____

Spiritual: _____

Relationships: _____

Free time: _____

Star Talents:
1. _____
2. _____
3. _____

Personal Strengths:
1. _____
2. _____
3. _____

Core Values:
1. _____
2. _____
3. _____

Useful Skills:
1. _____
2. _____
3. _____

What I Love to Do:
1. _____
2. _____
3. _____

As the star and producer of the movie of his/her life,
_____ is a person who
_____
_____
_____

My Vision in Life Is to:
_____
_____
_____
_____
_____
_____

Tagline for the movie: _____

Theme song:

My Purpose in Each Role I Play:

Family: _____

Education: _____

Work: _____

Physical: _____

Financial: _____

Spiritual: _____

Relationships: _____

Free time: _____

Star Talents:
1. _____
2. _____
3. _____

Personal Strengths:
1. _____
2. _____
3. _____

Core Values:
1. _____
2. _____
3. _____

Useful Skills:
1. _____
2. _____
3. _____

What I Love to Do:
1. _____
2. _____
3. _____

As the star and producer of the movie of his/her life,
_____ is a person who
_____
_____
_____

My Vision in Life Is to:
_____
_____
_____

Tagline for the movie: _____

Theme song: _____

My Purpose in Each Role I Play:

Family:

Education:

Work:

Physical:

Financial:

Spiritual:

Relationships:

Free time:

Tagline for the movie:

As the star and producer of the movie of his/her life,
_____ is a person who
_____

Star Talents:
1.
2.
3.

Personal Strengths:
1.
2.
3.

Core Values:
1.
2.
3.

Useful Skills:
1.
2.
3.

What I Love to Do:
1.
2.
3.

My Vision in Life Is to:

Theme song:

References and Recommended Reading

Acquinas, Thomas. "Summa Contra Gentiles," In *Happiness: Classic and Contemporary Readings in Philosophy,* ed. S. Cahn and C. Vitrano, 60-68. Oxford: Oxford University Press, 2007.

Adrienne, Carol. *The Purpose of Your Life.* New York: Eagle Book, 1998.

Anderson, Tom. *Your Place in the World: Creating a Life of Vision, Purpose, and Service.* n.p.: BookSurge, 2010.

Aristotle. "The Nicomachean Ethics," In *Happiness: Classic and Contemporary Readings in Philosophy,* ed. S. Cahn and C. Vitrano, 19-34. Oxford: Oxford University Press, 2007.

Baumeister, Roy F., and John Tierney. *Willpower: Rediscovering the Greatest Human Strength.* New York: Penguin Books, 2011.

Baumeister, Roy F., Kathleen D. Vohs, Jennifer L. Aaker, and Emily N. Garbinsky. "Some Key Differences between a Happy Life and a Meaningful Life." *Journal of Positive Psychology*, Vol. 8, Iss. 6, 2013

Bolles, Richard. *What Color Is Your Parachute?* New York: Ten Speed Press, 2014.

Braham, Barbara. *Finding Your Purpose: A Guide to Personal Fulfillment.* Mississauga, ON: Crisp Learning, 1995.

Brennfleck, Kevin, and Kay Marie Brennfleck. *Live Your Calling.* San Francisco: Jossey-Bass, 2004.

Brooks, David. "The Ultimate Spoiler Alert" [Commencement Address]. Dartmouth College: June 14, 2015, http://now.dartmouth.edu/2015/06/david-brooks-commencement-address

Buber, Martin. *I and Thou.* New York: Simon & Schuster, 1996.

Buechner, Frederick. *Wishful Thinking: A Theological ABC.* New York: Harper & Row, 1973.

Colbert, Stephen. "Stephen Colbert's Commencement Address." Knox College, June 2006, http://departments.knox.edu/newsarchive/news_events/2006/x12547.html

Cantor, N., and C. A. Sanderson. "Life Task Participation and Well-Being: The Importance of Taking Part in Daily Life." In *Well-Being: The Foundations of Hedonic Psychology*, ed. D. Kahneman, E. Diener, and N. Schwarz, 230–43. New York: Russell Sage Foundation, 1999.

Chaffee, D. S. "Truly Accomplished: Exploratory Study of Success Map Development." Honor's thesis, University of Central Florida, 2013.

Covey, Stephen. *The 7 Habits of Highly Effective People: Powerful Lessons in Personal Change.* New York: Simon & Schuster, 2013.

Crocker, Jennifer, and Amy Canevello. "Relationships and the Self: Egosystem and Ecosystem." In *APA Handbook of Personality and Social Psychology, Volume 3: Interpersonal Relations,* ed. M Mikulincer, P. Shaver, J. Simpson, and J. F. Dovidio, 93-116. Washington, DC: American Psychological Association, 2015.

Dahl, JoAnne, Jennifer C. Plumb, Ian Stewart, and Tobias Lundgren. *The Art and Science of Valuing in Psychotherapy.* Oakland: New Harbinger Publications, Inc, 2009.

Damon, William. *The Path to Purpose.* New York: Free Press, 2008.

Dik, Bryan J., and Ryan D. Duffy. *Make Your Job a Calling.* West Conshohocken, PA: Templeton Press, 2012.

Dunn, Elizabeth, and Michael Norton. "How Money Actually Buys Happiness." *Harvard Business Review* (June 28, 2013), https://hbr.org/2013/06/how-money-actually-buys-happiness/.

Dunn, Elizabeth, and Michael Norton. *Happy Money: The Science of Happier Spending.* New York: Simon & Schuester, 2013.

Emmons, R. A. *The Psychology of Ultimate Concerns: Motivation and Spirituality in Personality.* New York: Guilford Press, 1999.

Frankl, Victor, William J. Winslade, and Harold S. Kishner. *Man's Search for Meaning.* Cotchogue, NY: Buccaneer Books, Inc, 1992.

"Going to a Higher Authority." *USA Today,* May 28, 1999.

Gordon, Jon. *The Seed.* Hoboken: John Wiley & Sons, Inc, 2011.

Hahn, Thich Nhat. *Our Appointment with Life: Discourse on Living Happily in the Present Moment.* Berkeley: Parallax Press: 1990.

Hill, Patrick, et al. "Change You Can Believe In: Changes in Goal Setting during Emerging and Young Adulthood Predict Later Adult Well-Being." *Social Psychological and Personality Science* 2, no. 2 (March 2011): 123–31.

Hurst, Aaron. *The Purpose Economy.* Boise: Elevate, 2014.

Jay, Meg. *The Defining Decade: Why Your Twenties Matter—And How to Make the Most of Them.* New York: Twelve, 2012.

Keyes, C. L. M., D. Shmotkin, and C. D. Ryff. "Optimizing Well-Being: The Empirical Encounter of Two Traditions." *Journal of Personality and Social Psychology* 82 (2002): 1007–22.

Kobau, R., J. Sniezek, M. M. Zack, R. E. Lucas, and A. Burns. "Well-Being Assessment: An Evaluation of Well-Being Scales for Public Health and Population Estimates of Well-Being among U.S. Adults." *Applied Psychology: Health and Well-Being* 2, no. 3 (November 2010): 272–97.

Krumboltz, John D. "Happenstance Learning Theory." *Journal of Career Assessment* (December 30, 2008), http://web.stanford.edu/~jdk/HappenstanceLearningTheory2009.pdf

Leider, Richard. *The Power of Purpose: Find Meaning, Live Longer, Better.* Oakland: Berrett-Koehler Publishers, Inc, 2015.

Lewis, C. S. *Mere Christianity: A Revised and Amplified Edition, with a New Introduction of the Three Books, Broadcast Talks, Christian Behaviour, and Beyond Personality.* San Francisco: HarperOne, 2015.

Lore, Nicholas. *Now What? The Young Person's Guide to Choosing the Perfect Career.* New York: Fireside/Simon and Schuster, 2008.

Lore, Nicholas. *Pathfinder.* New York: Fireside, 1998.

McKay, Matthew, John P. Forsyth, and Georg H. Eifert. *Your Life on Purpose.* Oakland, CA: New Harbinger Publications, 2010.

Millman, Dan. *The Four Purposes of Life.* Novato, CA: H. J. Kramer/New World Library, 2011.

Parks, Sharon Daloz. *Big Questions, Worthy Dreams.* San Francisco: Jossey-Bass, 2011.

Pinker, Susan. *The Village Effect: How Face-to-Face Contact Can Make Us Healthier and Happier.* Toronto: Random House Canada, 2014.

Prelec, D., and R. Bodner. "Self-Signaling and Self-Control." In *Time and Decision: Economic and Psychological Perspectives on Intertemporal Choice*, ed. George Loewenstein, Daniel Read, and Roy F. Baumeister, 277–98. New York: Russell Sage Foundation.

Ryff, Carol D. "Happiness Is Everything, or Is It? Explorations on the Meaning of Psychological Well-Being." *Journal of Personality and Social Psychology* 57 (1989): 1069–81.

Scheier, M. F., C. Wrosch, A. Baum, S. Cohen, L. M. Martire, K. A. Matthews, R. Schulz, and B. Zdaniuk. "The Life Engagement Test: Assessing Purpose in Life." *Journal of Behavioral Medicine* 29 (2006): 291–98.

Schwartz, Shalom. "Are There Universal Aspects in the Structure and Contents of Human Values?." *Journal of Social Issues* 50 (1994): 19–45.

Schwartz, Shalom. "Universals in the Content and Structure of Values: Theory and Empirical Tests in 20 Countries." In *Advances in Experimental Social Psychology, Volume 25*, ed. M. Zanna, 1-65. New York: Academic Press, 1992.

Seligman, M. E. P. *Authentic Happiness.* New York: Free Press, 2002.

Seligman, M. E. P. *Flourish.* New York: Free Press, 2011.

Steger, Michael, Patricia Frazier, Shigehiro Oishi, and Matthew Kaler. "The Meaning in Life Questionnaire: Assessing the Presence of and Search for Meaning in Life." *Journal of Counseling Psychology* 50 (2006): 80-93.

Strecher, Victor J. *On Purpose: Lessons in Life and Health from the Frog, The Dung Beetle, and Julia.* Ann Arbor, MI: Dung Beetle Press, 2013.

Strecher, Victor J. *Life on Purpose: How Living for What Matters Most Changes Everything.* New York: HarperOne (2016).

Webster, Dan, and Randy Gravitt. *Finding Your Way: Discovering the Truth about You.* Holland: FYW Publishing, LLC, 2013.

Whelan, Christine B. *Generation WTF: From What the *^%$ to a Wise, Tenacious, and Fearless You.* West Conshohocken, PA: Templeton Press, 2011.

Wiseman, Richard. *59 Seconds: Change Your Life in Under a Minute.* New York: First Anchor Books, 2011.

Wrzesniewski, Amy, Clark McCauley, Paul Rozin, and Barry Schwartz. "Jobs, Careers, and Callings: People's Relations to Their Work." *Journal of Research in Personality* 31 (1997): 21–33.

Wrzesniewski, Amy, Justin M. Berg, and Jane E. Dutton. "Managing Yourself: Turn the Job You Have into the Job You Want." *Harvard Business Review* (June 2010 Issue), https://hbr.org/2010/06/managing-yourself-turn-the-job-you-have-into-the-job-you-want

About the Author

"NOT FOR SCHOOL BUT FOR LIFE WE LEARN," is Dr. Christine B. Whelan's professional motto. Her classes and writing embody Seneca's nod to the value of applied knowledge. *The Big Picture* is Dr. Whelan's most recent book translating academic research into step-by-step life learning.

Dr. Whelan is also the author of *Generation WTF: From "What the &%#$?" to a Wise, Tenacious, and Fearless You* (Templeton Press, 2011), *Marry Smart: The Intelligent Woman's Guide to True Love* (Simon & Schuster, 2009), and *Why Smart Men Marry Smart Women* (Simon & Schuster, 2006). She has been published in the *Wall Street Journal*, the *Washington Post* and the *New York Times*, among other national outlets. She has appeared on television programs and radio programs across the nation.

Dr. Whelan earned her masters and doctorate from the University of Oxford and currently teaches classes on happiness and well-being in the School of Human Ecology at the University of Wisconsin–Madison, where she also directs the Money, Relationships and Equality initiative.